chicken

chicken

MURDOCH BOOKS

contents

perfect poultry

It was Henry IV of France who famously said that he'd like to see that even the *peasants* in his realm didn't 'lack the means to have a chicken in the pot every Sunday'. It seems unbelievable that in times past, only the wealthy could afford to eat chicken regularly. Thank goodness those days are long gone and we can all enjoy it regularly.

This book is divided into chapters according to type: those that are 'light', those that are 'fast' and those that are 'slow'. 'Light' dishes are perfect for hot days, lazy days and occasions when snacking or grazing is on the agenda. Lighter offerings span soups, sandwiches and salads. 'Fast' dishes are those that can be whipped up in 30 minutes or less — a godsend for the busy cook. These recipes may skimp on time but they're not short on flavour. 'Slow' dishes are those which are not necessarily time-consuming to put together, but need long, gentle cooking in order for luscious flavours to form and mingle. In this category belong all those delicious, nourishing casseroles, stews, curries, bakes and fricassees that everyone seems to adore.

Whichever of these irresistible recipes best suit your needs, make sure you make them with the best chicken you can afford. Standard birds are fine but a free-range, corn-fed or fully organic one is even better. The old-fashioned chickeny flavour of a bird raised slowly and on a varied diet is a revelation. Just remember to raise your glass to the enlightened King Henry as you devour it!

light

Spicy chicken goujons

3 boneless, skinless chicken breasts,
   cut into thin strips
plain (all-purpose) flour, for coating
½ teaspoon ground turmeric
½ teaspoon ground coriander
½ teaspoon ground cumin
½ teaspoon chilli powder
oil, for deep-frying

Toss the chicken in the flour, shaking off the excess.

Mix together the turmeric, coriander, cumin, chilli powder and 1 teaspoon salt in a bowl and set aside until needed.

Fill a large heavy-based saucepan or deep-fryer one-third full of oil and heat to 180°C (350°F), or until a cube of bread dropped in the oil browns in 15 seconds. Cook the goujons in batches for 3 minutes, or until golden. Drain on crumpled paper towels and keep warm.

Toss the goujons in the spice mixture, shaking off the excess. Serve immediately.

MAKES ABOUT 30

Thai chicken balls

1 kg (2 lb 4 oz) minced (ground) chicken
80 g (2¾ oz/1 cup) fresh breadcrumbs
4 spring onions (scallions), sliced
1 tablespoon ground coriander
50 g (1¾ oz) chopped coriander (cilantro) leaves
3 tablespoons sweet chilli sauce, plus extra, to serve
1–2 tablespoons lemon juice
oil, for pan-frying

Preheat the oven to 200°C (400°F/Gas 6). Mix the chicken and breadcrumbs in a large bowl. Add the spring onion, ground and fresh coriander, chilli sauce and lemon juice and mix well. Using damp hands, roll the mixture into small balls.

Heat the oil in a deep frying pan and shallow-fry the chicken balls in batches over high heat until browned all over. Place them on a baking tray and bake for about 5 minutes, or until cooked through. Serve with sweet chilli sauce for dipping.

SERVES 6

Honey and mustard-glazed chicken drumettes

4 tablespoons oil
3 tablespoons honey
3 tablespoons soy sauce
3 tablespoons dijon mustard
3 tablespoons lemon juice
4 garlic cloves, crushed
24 chicken drumettes, trimmed (see Note)

Combine the oil, honey, soy sauce, mustard, lemon juice and garlic in a large non-metallic bowl. Add the chicken drumettes and coat in the marinade. Cover and marinate in the fridge for at least 2 hours, or overnight if time permits.

Preheat the oven to 200°C (400°F/Gas 6). Place the drumettes on a wire rack over a foil-lined baking tray. Bake, turning and brushing with the marinade 3–4 times, for 45 minutes, or until golden brown and cooked through. Serve immediately with paper towels or serviettes for sticky fingers.

MAKES 24

NOTE: Drumettes are the chicken wing with the wing tip removed.

Chicken san choy bau

1½ tablespoons vegetable oil
¼ teaspoon sesame oil
3 garlic cloves, crushed
3 teaspoons grated fresh ginger
6 spring onions (scallions), thinly sliced
500 g (1 lb 2 oz) minced (ground) chicken
100 g (3½ oz) drained water chestnuts, finely chopped
100 g (3½ oz) drained bamboo shoots, finely chopped
3 tablespoons oyster sauce, plus extra, to serve
2 teaspoons soy sauce
3 tablespoons sherry
1 teaspoon sugar
4 small witlof (chicory/Belgian endive) heads, bases trimmed

Heat a wok to very hot, add the oils and swirl to coat the side. Add the garlic, ginger and half the spring onion and stir-fry over high heat for 1 minute. Add the chicken and continue cooking for 3–4 minutes, or until just cooked, breaking up any lumps with a fork.

Add the water chestnuts, bamboo shoots, oyster and soy sauces, sherry, sugar and the remaining spring onion. Cook for 2–3 minutes, or until the liquid thickens a little.

Allow the mixture to cool slightly before dividing among the witlof leaves; you will need about 2 heaped teaspoons per leaf. Drizzle with a little oyster sauce and serve immediately.

MAKES ABOUT 36

Macadamia-crusted
chicken strips

12 chicken tenderloins, larger ones halved, cut into strips
seasoned plain (all-purpose) flour, to dust
2 eggs, lightly beaten
250 g (9 oz) macadamia nuts, finely chopped
165 g (5¾ oz/2 cups) fresh breadcrumbs
oil, for deep-frying

Dust the chicken strips with the flour, then dip them in the egg and, finally, coat them in the combined nuts and breadcrumbs. Refrigerate for at least 30 minutes to firm up.

Fill a large heavy-based saucepan or deep-fryer one-third full of oil and heat to 180°C (350°F), or until a cube of bread dropped in the oil browns in 15 seconds. Cook the chicken in batches for 2–3 minutes, or until golden brown all over, taking care not to burn the nuts. Drain on crumpled paper towels. Serve warm.

MAKES 24

Chicken liver parfait

35 g (1¼ oz) butter
2 French shallots, sliced
500 g (1 lb 2 oz) chicken livers, trimmed
3 tablespoons thick (double/heavy) cream
1 tablespoon cognac or brandy
48 Melba toasts
8 cornichons (baby gherkins), thinly sliced
   on the diagonal

Heat a large frying pan over medium heat. Melt the butter, then add the sliced shallots to the pan and cook, stirring, for 4–5 minutes, or until they are soft and transparent. Use a slotted spoon to transfer them to a food processor.

In the same pan, add the chicken livers and cook in batches over high heat, stirring, for 4–5 minutes, or until seared on the outside but still pink and quite soft on the inside. Add to the food processor along with 2 tablespoons of the pan juices, the cream, cognac and some salt and pepper. Blend for 4–5 minutes, or until quite smooth. Push through a fine sieve to remove any remaining lumps. Transfer to a bowl or serving dish, put plastic wrap directly on the surface of the mixture and refrigerate for at least 4 hours, or until cold.

To serve, spoon a heaped teaspoon of parfait onto each Melba toast and top with a slice of cornichon. Alternatively, leave the parfait in the serving dish, supply a small knife and allow guests to help themselves.

MAKES 48

Mediterranean
chicken skewers

2 large boneless, skinless chicken breasts,
    cut into 32 cubes
24 cherry tomatoes
6 cap mushrooms, quartered
2 garlic cloves, crushed
zest of 1 lemon, grated
2 tablespoons lemon juice
2 tablespoons olive oil
1 tablespoon oregano, chopped
lemon wedges, to serve

Soak eight wooden skewers in water to prevent scorching. Thread a piece of chicken onto each skewer, followed by a tomato, then a piece of mushroom. Repeat twice for each skewer and finish with a piece of chicken. Put the skewers in a shallow, non-metallic dish.

Combine the garlic, lemon zest, lemon juice, olive oil and chopped oregano, pour over the skewers and toss well. Marinate for at least 2 hours, or overnight if time permits.

Lightly oil a barbecue chargrill plate or flat plate and heat it to high direct heat. Cook the skewers for 4 minutes on each side, basting occasionally, until the chicken is cooked and the tomatoes have shrivelled slightly. Serve with lemon wedges to squeeze over the skewers.

MAKES 8

Money bags

1 tablespoon oil
4 red Asian shallots, chopped
2 garlic cloves, crushed
1 tablespoon grated fresh ginger
300 g (10½ oz) minced (ground)
    chicken
3 tablespoons chopped peanuts
3 tablespoons finely chopped
    coriander (cilantro) leaves
3 teaspoons fish sauce
2 teaspoons soy sauce

2 teaspoons lime juice
2 teaspoons grated palm sugar
    (jaggery) or soft brown sugar
30 won ton wrappers
oil, for deep-frying
garlic chives, for tying

Dipping sauce
2 teaspoons sugar
125 ml (4 fl oz/½ cup) vinegar
1 red chilli, seeded and chopped

Heat the oil in a frying pan over medium heat. Add the shallots, garlic and ginger and cook for 1–2 minutes. Add the chicken and cook for 4 minutes, or until cooked, breaking up any lumps with a wooden spoon. Stir in the peanuts, coriander, fish sauce, soy sauce, lime juice and sugar and cook, stirring, for 1–2 minutes. Cool.

Form your thumb and index finger into a circle, and place a won ton wrapper on top. Put 2 teaspoons of the filling in the centre, then brush the edge with water. Push the mixture down firmly with your free hand, tightening the circle of your thumb and index finger at the same time, encasing the mixture in the wrapper. Trim.

Fill a large heavy-based saucepan or deep-fryer one-third full of oil and heat to 190°C (375°F), or until a cube of bread dropped in the oil browns in 10 seconds. Cook in batches for 30–60 seconds, or until golden. Drain. Tie the 'neck' of the money bags with the chives.

To make the dipping sauce, dissolve the sugar and 1 teaspoon salt in the vinegar. Add the chilli and mix. Serve the sauce in a small bowl alongside the money bags.

MAKES 30

Crunchy Thai chicken and peanut cakes

3 teaspoons grated palm sugar (jaggery) or soft brown sugar
1 tablespoon fish sauce
350 g (12 oz) minced (ground) chicken
120 g (4¼ oz/¾ cup) peanuts, toasted and chopped
40 g (1½ oz/½ cup) fresh breadcrumbs
1 tablespoon Thai red curry paste
1 tablespoon lime juice
3 makrut (kaffir lime) leaves, very finely shredded
2 tablespoons sweet chilli sauce, plus extra, to serve
2 tablespoons chopped coriander (cilantro) leaves
125 ml (4 fl oz/½ cup) oil
1 banana leaf, cut into 24 x 5 cm (2 inch) square pieces

Dissolve the sugar in the fish sauce, then put in a bowl with the chicken, peanuts, breadcrumbs, curry paste, lime juice, lime leaves, sweet chilli sauce and coriander. Mix well. Divide the mixture into 24 small balls — they will be quite soft. Flatten the balls into discs about 1.5 cm (⅝ inch) thick. Lay them in a single layer on a tray, cover with plastic wrap and refrigerate for 30 minutes.

Heat the oil in a heavy-based frying pan and cook the chicken cakes in batches for 2–3 minutes on each side, or until firm and golden. Drain on crumpled paper towels.

Place a chicken cake on each square of banana leaf and top with a dash of sweet chilli sauce. Secure with a toothpick for easier serving.

MAKES 24

Deep-fried chicken balls

50 g (1¾ oz) dried rice vermicelli
500 g (1 lb 2 oz) minced
   (ground) chicken
3 garlic cloves, finely chopped
1 tablespoon chopped fresh
   ginger
1 red chilli, seeded and finely
   chopped
1 egg, lightly beaten
2 spring onions (scallions), thinly
   sliced
4 tablespoons chopped
   coriander (cilantro) leaves

4 tablespoons plain
   (all-purpose) flour
4 tablespoons finely chopped
   water chestnuts
oil, for deep-frying

Dipping sauce
125 ml (4 fl oz/½ cup) sweet
   chilli sauce
125 ml (4 fl oz/½ cup) soy sauce
1 tablespoon Chinese rice wine

Cover the vermicelli with boiling water and soak for 6–7 minutes. Drain, then cut into short lengths.

Combine the chicken, garlic, ginger, chilli, egg, spring onion, coriander, flour and water chestnuts in a large bowl. Mix in the vermicelli and season with salt. Refrigerate for 30 minutes. Roll heaped tablespoons of mixture into balls.

Fill a large heavy-based saucepan or deep-fryer one-third full of oil and heat to 180°C (350°F), or until a cube of bread dropped in the oil browns in 15 seconds. Deep-fry the balls in batches for 2 minutes, or until golden brown and cooked through. Drain on crumpled paper towels. Keep warm.

To make the dipping sauce, mix the sweet chilli sauce, soy sauce and rice wine. Serve in a small bowl alongside the hot chicken balls.

MAKES ABOUT 30

Spicy chicken sausage rolls

500 g (1 lb 2 oz) minced (ground) chicken
1 teaspoon ground cumin
1 teaspoon ground coriander
2 tablespoons sweet chilli sauce, plus extra, to serve
2 tablespoons chopped coriander (cilantro) leaves
80 g (2¾ oz/1 cup) fresh breadcrumbs
2 sheets frozen puff pastry, thawed
1 egg, lightly beaten
1 tablespoon sesame seeds

Preheat the oven to 200°C (400°F/Gas 6). Combine the chicken, cumin, coriander, chilli sauce, coriander leaves and breadcrumbs in a bowl.

Spread the mixture along one edge of each pastry sheet and roll up to conceal the filling. Place the rolls, seam side down, on a tray lined with baking paper, brush lightly with the beaten egg and sprinkle with sesame seeds. Bake for 30 minutes, or until golden and cooked through. Slice the rolls and serve with sweet chilli sauce for dipping.

SERVES 6–8

Spinach and chicken salad with sesame dressing

450 g (1 lb) baby English spinach leaves
1 Lebanese (short) cucumber, peeled and diced
4 spring onions (scallions), shredded
2 carrots, cut into matchsticks
2 boneless, skinless chicken breasts, cooked
2 tablespoons tahini
2 tablespoons lime juice
3 teaspoons sesame oil
1 teaspoon sugar
pinch chilli flakes
2 tablespoons sesame seeds
1 large handful coriander (cilantro) leaves

Put the spinach in a large bowl. Scatter the cucumber, spring onion and carrot over the top. Shred the chicken breast into long pieces and scatter it over the vegetables.

Mix together the tahini, lime juice, sesame oil, sugar and chilli flakes, then add salt to taste. Drizzle this dressing over the salad.

Cook the sesame seeds in a dry frying pan over low heat for 1–2 minutes, stirring often. When they start to brown and smell toasted, tip them over the salad. Scatter the coriander leaves over the top. Toss the salad just before serving.

SERVES 4

Chicken Waldorf salad

750 ml (26 fl oz/3 cups) chicken stock
2 boneless, skinless chicken breasts
2 red apples
2 green apples
2 celery stalks, sliced
100 g (3½ oz/1 cup) walnuts, toasted
125 g (4½ oz/½ cup) whole-egg mayonnaise
3 tablespoons sour cream
½ teaspoon chopped tarragon
1 baby cos (romaine) lettuce

Bring the stock to the boil in a medium saucepan. Remove from the heat, add the chicken to the stock, then cover and allow to cool in the liquid for 10 minutes, by which time the chicken should be cooked. Test by touching with your finger — the chicken should feel quite springy.

Slice the apples into matchsticks. Shred the chicken breasts and put in a large bowl with the apple, celery, walnuts, mayonnaise, sour cream and tarragon. Season with salt and freshly ground black pepper, and toss well to combine. Separate the lettuce leaves and arrange them in the base of a serving bowl. Pile the Waldorf salad over the lettuce and serve.

SERVES 4

Chicken with rocket and cannellini bean salad

4 tablespoons lemon juice

3 garlic cloves, crushed

1 teaspoon soft brown sugar

3 tablespoons finely chopped basil

125 ml (4 fl oz/½ cup) olive oil

4 boneless, skinless chicken breasts

400 g (14 oz) tin cannellini beans, drained and rinsed

100 g (3½ oz) baby rocket (arugula) leaves

Lightly oil a barbecue chargrill plate or flat plate and heat it to high direct heat. Whisk together the lemon juice, garlic, sugar, basil and olive oil, and season lightly with salt and pepper. Pour one-third of the dressing over the chicken to coat. Cook the chicken for 4 minutes on each side, or until cooked through.

Meanwhile, combine the beans and rocket with the remaining dressing, toss well and season. Slice the chicken and serve over the rocket and bean salad.

SERVES 4

Vietnamese chicken and bean sprout salad

2 boneless, skinless chicken breasts or 4 thighs, cooked
2 tablespoons lime juice
1½ tablespoons fish sauce
¼ teaspoon sugar
1–2 bird's eye chillies, finely chopped
1 garlic clove, crushed
2 French shallots, thinly sliced
2 handfuls bean sprouts, trimmed
1 large handful shredded Chinese cabbage (wong bok)
4 tablespoons Vietnamese mint or mint, finely chopped

Take the flesh off the chicken bones and shred it. Discard the skin and bones.

Mix together the lime juice, fish sauce, sugar, chilli, garlic and sliced shallots.

Bring a saucepan of water to the boil and throw in the bean sprouts. After 10 seconds, drain them and rinse under cold water to stop them cooking any longer.

Mix the bean sprouts with the Chinese cabbage, mint and chicken. Pour the dressing over the salad and toss everything well before serving.

SERVES 4

Chicken sandwich

2 boneless, skinless chicken breasts,
   halved horizontally
2 tablespoons olive oil
2 tablespoons lemon juice
4 large pieces ciabatta, halved horizontally
1 garlic clove, halved
mayonnaise, to spread
1 avocado, sliced
2 tomatoes, sliced
1 large handful rocket (arugula) leaves,
   long stems snapped off

Pound each chicken breast between two sheets of plastic wrap with a mallet or rolling pin until about 1 cm (½ inch) thick.

Heat the oil in a frying pan, add the chicken pieces and fry them on both sides for 2–3 minutes, or until they turn brown and are cooked through. Sprinkle with the lemon juice, then take the chicken out of the pan. Add the bread to the pan, cut side down, and cook for 1 minute, pressing down on it to flatten it and help soak up any juices.

Take the bread out of the pan, rub the cut side of the garlic over the surface, then spread all the pieces with a generous amount of mayonnaise.

Put a piece of chicken on four of the bread pieces, season and then layer with the avocado and tomato, seasoning as you go. Finish with the rocket and the tops of the bread, then serve.

SERVES 4

Minced chicken salad

1 tablespoon jasmine rice
2 teaspoons oil
400 g (14 oz) minced (ground) chicken
2 tablespoons fish sauce
1 lemongrass stem, white part only, finely chopped
4 tablespoons chicken stock
3 tablespoons lime juice
4 spring onions (scallions), thinly sliced on the diagonal
4 red Asian shallots, sliced
2 large handfuls coriander (cilantro) leaves, finely chopped
2 large handfuls mint, shredded
200 g (7 oz) lettuce, shredded
3 tablespoons peanuts, toasted and chopped
1 small red chilli, sliced
lime wedges, to serve

Heat a frying pan. Add the rice and dry-fry over low heat for 3 minutes, or until lightly golden. Grind in a mortar and pestle to a fine powder.

Heat a wok to medium, add the oil and swirl to coat the side. Add the chicken and cook for 4 minutes, or until it changes colour, breaking up any lumps. Add the fish sauce, lemongrass and stock and cook for a further 10 minutes. Remove from the wok and allow to cool.

Add the lime juice, spring onion, sliced shallots, coriander, mint and ground rice to the chicken mixture. Mix well.

Arrange the lettuce on a serving platter and top with the chicken mixture. Sprinkle with the nuts and chilli, and serve with lime wedges.

SERVES 6

Won ton chicken ravioli with a Thai dressing

400 g (14 oz) minced (ground) chicken

2 spring onions (scallions), finely chopped

3 makrut (kaffir lime) leaves, very finely shredded

2 tablespoons sweet chilli sauce

3 tablespoons chopped coriander (cilantro) leaves

1½ teaspoons sesame oil

2 teaspoons grated lime zest

270 g (9½ oz) packet won ton wrappers

125 ml (4 fl oz/½ cup) fish sauce

2 tablespoons grated palm sugar (jaggery) or soft brown sugar

1 tablespoon vegetable oil

1 tablespoon lime juice

finely chopped red chilli, to garnish

chopped coriander (cilantro) leaves, to garnish

Combine the chicken, spring onion, lime leaves, chilli sauce, coriander, sesame oil and lime zest in a bowl.

Place a tablespoon of the chicken mixture in the centre of a won ton wrapper, brush the edges lightly with water and top with another wrapper, pressing down firmly around the edges to stop the ravioli from opening during cooking. Repeat with the remaining filling and won ton wrappers.

Cook the ravioli in batches in a large saucepan of boiling water for 5 minutes, or until *al dente* and the chicken is cooked, then drain well and place on serving plates.

Combine the fish sauce, sugar, vegetable oil and lime juice in a bowl. Pour over the ravioli and garnish with the chilli and coriander before serving.

SERVES 4

Satay chicken skewers

1 garlic clove, crushed
2 teaspoons finely grated fresh
   ginger
3 teaspoons fish sauce
500 g (1 lb 2 oz) boneless,
   skinless chicken thighs,
   cut into 1 cm (½ inch)
   wide strips

Satay sauce
2 teaspoons oil
4 red Asian shallots, finely
   chopped
4 garlic cloves, crushed

2 teaspoons finely chopped
   fresh ginger
2 small red chillies, seeded and
   finely chopped
125 g (4½ oz/½ cup) crunchy
   peanut butter
185 ml (6 fl oz/¾ cup) coconut
   milk
2 teaspoons soy sauce
2 teaspoons grated palm sugar
   (jaggery) or soft brown sugar
1½ tablespoons fish sauce
1 makrut (kaffir lime) leaf
1½ tablespoons lime juice

Soak 12 wooden skewers in water to prevent scorching. Combine the garlic, ginger and fish sauce in a large non-metallic bowl. Add the chicken and coat it in the marinade. Cover and marinate in the fridge for 1 hour.

To make the satay sauce, heat the oil in a saucepan over medium heat, then add the shallot, garlic, ginger and chilli. Stir the mixture constantly with a wooden spoon for 5 minutes, or until the shallots are golden. Reduce the heat to low, add the remaining sauce ingredients and simmer for 10 minutes, or until the sauce has thickened. Remove the lime leaf and keep the sauce warm while you cook the chicken.

Lightly oil a barbecue chargrill plate and heat it to medium–high direct heat. Thread two or three chicken strips onto each skewer, and cook for 10 minutes, or until cooked through, turning after 5 minutes. Serve with the satay sauce.

SERVES 4

Wild rice and chicken salad with Asian dressing

190 g (6¾ oz/1 cup) wild rice
200 g (7 oz/1 cup) jasmine rice
1 Chinese barbecued roast
  chicken (see Note)
3 tablespoons chopped mint
3 tablespoons chopped
  coriander (cilantro) leaves
1 large Lebanese (short)
  cucumber

6 spring onions (scallions)
80 g (2¾ oz/½ cup) peanuts,
  toasted and roughly chopped
4 tablespoons mirin
2 tablespoons Chinese rice wine
1 tablespoon soy sauce
1 tablespoon lime juice
2 tablespoons sweet chilli sauce,
  plus extra, to serve

Bring a large saucepan of water to the boil and add 1 teaspoon of salt and the wild rice. Cook for 30 minutes, add the jasmine rice and cook for a further 10 minutes, or until tender. Drain the rice, refresh under cold water and drain again.

Shred the chicken (the skin as well) into bite-sized pieces, put in a large bowl and add the mint and coriander. Cut the cucumber through the centre (do not peel) and slice thinly on the diagonal. Slice the spring onions on the diagonal. Add the cucumber, spring onion, rice and peanuts to the bowl with the chicken.

Mix together the mirin, rice wine, soy, lime juice and sweet chilli sauce in a small bowl, pour over the salad and toss to combine. Pile the salad onto serving platters and serve with extra chilli sauce.

SERVES 8

NOTE: It is important to use a Chinese barbecued chicken, available from Chinese barbecue shops. The flavours of five-spice and soy used to cook it will add to the flavour of the dish.

Chicken with spinach and raspberry salad

3 tablespoons raspberry vinegar
2 tablespoons lime juice
2 garlic cloves, crushed
2 tablespoons chopped oregano
1 teaspoon soft brown sugar
2 small red chillies, finely chopped
125 ml (4 fl oz/½ cup) virgin olive oil
4 boneless, skinless chicken breasts
1 teaspoon dijon mustard
200 g (7 oz) baby English spinach leaves
250 g (9 oz) raspberries

Combine 2 tablespoons of the raspberry vinegar, the lime juice, crushed garlic, 1 tablespoon of the oregano, the sugar, chilli and 3 tablespoons of the oil in a large non-metallic bowl. Add the chicken and coat in the marinade. Cover and marinate for 2 hours in the fridge.

Preheat the oven to 180°C (350°F/Gas 4). Heat a chargrill pan and cook the chicken for 3 minutes on each side, then place on a baking tray and bake for a further 5 minutes, or until cooked through. Allow the chicken to rest for 5 minutes, then cut each breast into five strips on the diagonal.

To make the dressing, combine the remaining oil, vinegar and oregano with the mustard, ¼ teaspoon salt and freshly ground black pepper and mix well. Toss the spinach and raspberries with half of the dressing. Top with the chicken and drizzle with the remaining dressing before serving.

SERVES 4

Chicken and fresh tzatziki wrap

½ telegraph (long) cucumber, seeded and grated
100 g (3½ oz) low-fat natural yoghurt
¼ teaspoon lemon juice
1 tablespoon chopped mint
4 boneless, skinless chicken thighs
pinch paprika
4 sheets lavash or other flat bread (see Note)
4 large butter lettuce leaves

Sprinkle the grated cucumber with ½ teaspoon salt. Leave the cucumber for 10 minutes, then drain and mix with the yoghurt, lemon juice and mint. Season to taste with salt and freshly ground black pepper.

Preheat the grill (broiler). Pound each chicken thigh between two sheets of plastic wrap with a mallet or rolling pin until 2 cm (¾ inch) thick. Season the chicken with salt and pepper and sprinkle with the paprika. Grill the chicken for about 6 minutes on each side, or until cooked through. Slice on the diagonal.

Lay out the lavash breads and place a large butter lettuce leaf on each. Spread each with one-quarter of the tzatziki, then top with a sliced chicken thigh. Roll up, folding one end closed. Wrap in baking paper to serve.

MAKES 4

NOTE: If you can't find lavash, use any thin, flat bread that will roll up easily.

Smoked chicken and pasta salad

Dressing
1 tablespoon balsamic vinegar
150 ml (5 fl oz) olive oil
1 tablespoon lemon juice
3 tablespoons wholegrain
  mustard

200 g (7 oz) bucatini
450 g (1 lb) good-quality smoked
  chicken breasts (see Note)
8 small radishes
2 small Fuji apples
4 spring onions (scallions),
  thinly sliced
35 g (1¼ oz) rocket (arugula)
  leaves

To make the dressing, combine the vinegar, olive oil, lemon juice and mustard in a screw-top jar, and shake well to combine. Season to taste with salt and pepper.

Bring a large saucepan of salted water to the boil and cook the pasta according to the packet instructions until *al dente*. Drain, rinse under cold water and drain again. Toss one-third of the dressing through the bucatini and set aside for 30 minutes.

Cut the chicken breasts on the diagonal and put in a large bowl. Thinly slice the radishes and add to the chicken. Quarter, core and cube the apples without peeling them, and add to the chicken with the sliced spring onion and rocket. Pour in the remaining dressing and toss lightly.

Gently mix the pasta with the smoked chicken until well combined. Divide the salad among four serving dishes and serve.

SERVES 4

NOTE: Smoked chicken often has a dark skin. You may wish to remove this to improve the appearance of the salad.

Avgolemono with chicken

1 carrot, chopped
1 large leek, white part only, chopped
2 bay leaves
2 boneless, skinless chicken breasts
2 litres (70 fl oz/8 cups) chicken stock
4 tablespoons short-grain rice
3 eggs, separated
4 tablespoons lemon juice
2 tablespoons chopped parsley
40 g (1½ oz) butter, chopped

Put the carrot, leek, bay leaves, chicken and stock in a large saucepan. Bring to the boil over high heat, then reduce the heat and simmer for 10–15 minutes, or until the chicken is cooked.

Strain the stock through a fine sieve and return to the cleaned pan. Discard the vegetables and bay leaf, and set the chicken aside. Add the rice to the stock, bring to the boil, then reduce the heat and simmer for 15 minutes, or until tender. Meanwhile, cut the chicken into 1 cm (½ inch) cubes.

Whisk the egg whites in a clean, dry bowl until firm peaks form. Beat in the yolks until light and creamy, whisk in the lemon juice, then 250 ml (9 fl oz/1 cup) of the soup. Remove the soup from the heat and gradually whisk in the egg mixture. Add the chicken and stir over low heat for 2 minutes — do not boil or the egg will scramble. Serve at once with a sprinkle of parsley and dot of butter.

SERVES 4

NOTE: This soup will not stand well — make just before serving.

Chicken and spinach risoni soup

1 tablespoon olive oil
1 leek, white part only, quartered lengthways
 and thinly sliced
2 garlic cloves, crushed
1 teaspoon ground cumin
1.5 litres (52 fl oz/6 cups) chicken stock
2 boneless, skinless chicken breasts
205 g (7¼ oz/1 cup) risoni
150 g (5½ oz) baby English spinach leaves,
 roughly chopped
1 tablespoon chopped dill
2 teaspoons lemon juice

Heat the oil in a large saucepan over low heat. Add the leek and cook for 8–10 minutes, or until soft. Add the garlic and cumin and cook for 1 minute further. Pour the stock into the saucepan, increase the heat to high and bring to the boil. Reduce the heat to low, add the chicken and simmer, covered, for 8 minutes. Remove the chicken from the broth, allow to cool slightly, then shred.

Stir the risoni into the broth and simmer for 12 minutes, or until *al dente*.

Return the chicken to the broth along with the spinach and dill. Simmer for 2 minutes, or until the spinach has wilted. Stir in the lemon juice, season to taste with salt and freshly ground black pepper and serve.

SERVES 4

Chicken with ponzu sauce and somen noodles

Ponzu sauce

1 tablespoon lemon juice

1 tablespoon lime juice

1 tablespoon rice vinegar

1 tablespoon tamari

1½ tablespoons mirin

2½ tablespoons Japanese soy
  sauce

5 cm (2 inch) piece kombu (kelp),
  wiped with a damp cloth

1 tablespoon bonito flakes

900 g (2 lb) skinless chicken
  thighs, trimmed and halved
  across the bone

10 cm (4 inch) piece kombu (kelp)

200 g (7 oz) dried somen noodles

250 g (9 oz) fresh shiitake
  mushrooms (cut into smaller
  pieces if too large)

1 carrot, thinly sliced

300 g (10½ oz) baby English
  spinach leaves

To make the sauce, combine all the ingredients in a non-metallic bowl. Cover with plastic wrap and refrigerate overnight, then strain through a fine sieve.

Put the chicken and kombu in a large saucepan with 875 ml (30 fl oz/3½ cups) water. Simmer over medium heat for 20 minutes, or until the chicken is cooked, skimming the scum off the surface. Remove the chicken and strain the broth. Return the broth and chicken to the clean pan. Cover and cook over low heat for 15 minutes.

Meanwhile, cook the noodles in a large saucepan of boiling water for 2 minutes, or until tender. Drain and rinse under cold running water.

Add the mushrooms and carrot to the chicken and cook for 5 minutes. Add the noodles, then top with the spinach leaves. Cover and cook for 2 minutes, or until the spinach has just wilted. Stir in 4–6 tablespoons of the ponzu sauce and serve.

SERVES 4

Thai-style chicken and coconut soup

2 lemongrass stems, white part finely chopped, stem ends reserved and halved
6 garlic cloves, chopped
3 red Asian shallots, chopped
8 black peppercorns
1 teaspoon Thai red curry paste
250 ml (9 fl oz/1 cup) coconut cream
400 ml (14 fl oz) coconut milk
400 ml (14 fl oz) chicken stock
2½ tablespoons thinly sliced fresh galangal

7 makrut (kaffir lime) leaves, shredded
400 g (14 oz) boneless, skinless chicken breasts or thighs, thinly sliced
2 tablespoons lime juice
2 tablespoons fish sauce
1 teaspoon grated palm sugar (jaggery) or soft brown sugar
3 tablespoons coriander (cilantro) leaves
1 small red chilli, thinly sliced

Process the chopped lemongrass, garlic, shallots, peppercorns and curry paste in a food processor to form a paste.

Heat a wok over low heat, add the coconut cream, increase the heat to high and bring to the boil. Add the paste and cook, stirring, for 5 minutes. Add the coconut milk and stock, return to the boil and add the sliced galangal, the lime leaves and reserved lemongrass stems. Reduce the heat and simmer for 5 minutes.

Add the chicken and simmer for 8 minutes, or until cooked. Stir in the lime juice, fish sauce, sugar, coriander leaves and chilli. Serve immediately.

SERVES 4

fast

Chicken gumbo

30 g (1 oz) butter
2 bacon slices, thinly sliced
1 small onion, chopped
2 garlic cloves, chopped
1 small green capsicum
  (pepper), diced
¼ teaspoon cayenne pepper
600 g (1 lb 5 oz) boneless,
  skinless chicken breasts,
  cut into bite-sized cubes
¼ teaspoon saffron threads,
  soaked in 2 tablespoons
  warm water
1 tablespoon brandy
1 tablespoon tomato paste
  (concentrated purée)

2 tablespoons plain
  (all-purpose) flour
1 litre (35 fl oz/4 cups) chicken
  stock
150 g (5½ oz/¾ cup) basmati rice
1 tablespoon olive oil
400 g (14 oz) raw small prawns
  (shrimp), peeled and
  deveined, tails intact
300 g (10½ oz) okra, thickly
  sliced
2 tablespoons pouring
  (whipping) cream
3 tablespoons chopped flat-leaf
  (Italian) parsley
½ teaspoon Tabasco sauce

Melt the butter in a large saucepan over medium heat, add the bacon, onion, garlic, capsicum, cayenne and chicken, and cook, stirring, for 5–8 minutes, or until golden.

Stir in the saffron and soaking liquid, the brandy, tomato paste and flour, and cook, stirring constantly, for 3 minutes. Gradually add the stock and bring to the boil. Add the rice, then reduce the heat to low and simmer gently for 10 minutes.

Meanwhile, heat the olive oil in a separate saucepan, add the prawns and okra, and toss quickly together for 1–2 minutes, or until the prawns change colour. Add to the gumbo, then stir in the cream, parsley and Tabasco, and heat for 1–2 minutes. Serve in deep bowls with corn bread.

SERVES 4–6

Miso yakitori chicken

3 tablespoons yellow or red miso paste
2 tablespoons sugar
3 tablespoons sake
2 tablespoons mirin
1 kg (2 lb 4 oz) boneless chicken thighs
   (skin on), cut into bite-sized cubes
1 telegraph (long) cucumber, seeded and
   cut into 2 cm (¾ inch) batons
2 spring onions (scallions), cut into 2 cm
   (¾ inch) lengths

Soak 12 wooden skewers in water to prevent scorching. Put the miso, sugar, sake and mirin in a small saucepan over medium heat and cook, stirring well, for 2 minutes, or until the sauce is smooth and the sugar has dissolved completely.

Thread the chicken, cucumber and spring onion pieces alternately onto the skewers — you should have three pieces of chicken, three pieces of cucumber and three pieces of spring onion per skewer.

Lightly oil a barbecue chargrill plate or flat plate and heat it to high direct heat. Cook the skewers, turning occasionally, for 10 minutes, or until the chicken is almost cooked. Just before the chicken is cooked, brush the miso sauce over the skewers, then turn them over. Keep brushing and turning until the chicken and vegetables are cooked. Serve immediately with rice and salad.

SERVES 4

Salt and pepper
chicken with Asian greens and oyster sauce

4 tablespoons plain (all-purpose) flour
¾ teaspoon Chinese five-spice
1½ teaspoons sea salt
1 teaspoon ground white pepper
750 g (1 lb 10 oz) boneless, skinless chicken breasts,
   cut into thin strips
145 ml (4¾ fl oz) oil
1.25 kg (2 lb 12 oz) mixed Asian greens
125 ml (4 fl oz/½ cup) oyster sauce

Combine the flour, five-spice, salt and pepper in a large bowl. Toss the chicken strips in the flour until well coated. Heat 3 tablespoons of the oil in a large frying pan over medium–high heat. Add the chicken in three batches and cook, turning, for about 3 minutes, or until browned. Drain on crumpled paper towels and keep warm.

Heat the remaining oil and cook the mixed Asian greens over medium–high heat for 1–2 minutes. Add the oyster sauce and toss through. Serve on a bed of jasmine rice topped with the chicken strips.

SERVES 4

Cajun chicken with fresh tomato and corn salsa

2 corn cobs
2 vine-ripened tomatoes, diced
1 Lebanese (short) cucumber, diced
2 tablespoons roughly chopped coriander
   (cilantro) leaves
4 boneless, skinless chicken breasts
3 tablespoons Cajun seasoning
2 tablespoons lime juice
lime wedges, to serve

Cook the corn cobs in a saucepan of boiling water for 5 minutes, or until tender. Remove the kernels using a sharp knife and put in a bowl with the tomato, cucumber and coriander. Season and mix well.

Lightly oil a barbecue chargrill plate or flat plate and heat it to medium direct heat. Pound each chicken breast between two sheets of plastic wrap with a mallet or rolling pin until 2 cm (¾ inch) thick. Lightly coat the chicken with the Cajun seasoning and shake off any excess. Cook for 5 minutes on each side, or until just cooked through.

Just before serving, stir the lime juice into the salsa. Place a chicken breast on each plate and spoon the salsa on the side. Serve with the lime wedges, a green salad and crusty bread.

SERVES 4

Green chicken and eggplant curry

250 ml (9 fl oz/1 cup) coconut cream
4 tablespoons green curry paste
8 boneless, skinless chicken thighs or 4 breasts,
    cut into bite-sized cubes
250 ml (9 fl oz/1 cup) coconut milk
4 Thai eggplants (aubergines) or ½ purple eggplant
    (aubergine), cut into chunks
2 tablespoons grated palm sugar (jaggery)
    or soft brown sugar
2 tablespoons fish sauce
4 makrut (kaffir lime) leaves, torn
1 handful Thai basil
1–2 large red chillies, sliced
coconut milk or cream, for drizzling

Put the coconut cream in a wok, bring to the boil over high heat and cook for
10 minutes, or until the oil separates.

Add the curry paste, stir for 1 minute, then add the chicken. Cook the chicken until
it turns opaque, then add the coconut milk and eggplant. Cook for 1–2 minutes,
or until the eggplant is tender. Add the sugar, fish sauce, lime leaves and half of the
basil, then mix together.

Garnish with the rest of the basil, the chilli and a drizzle of coconut milk or cream.
Serve with steamed rice.

SERVES 4

Thai red chicken with Chinese broccoli

1 tablespoon Thai red curry paste
250 ml (9 fl oz/1 cup) coconut
   cream
3 makrut (kaffir lime) leaves
4 boneless, skinless chicken
   breasts, tenderloin removed
250 ml (9 fl oz/1 cup) chicken
   stock

1 tablespoon soy sauce
1 garlic clove, bruised
2 x 2 cm (¾ x ¾ inch) piece
   fresh ginger, bruised
750 g (1 lb 10 oz) Chinese
   broccoli (gai larn), washed
   and tied in a bunch
coriander (cilantro) sprigs

Combine the curry paste, coconut cream and lime leaves in a large non-metallic bowl. Add the chicken and coat it in the marinade. Cover and marinate for 10 minutes, or overnight if time permits.

Put the chicken stock, soy sauce, garlic and ginger in a small saucepan and boil for 5 minutes, or until it is reduced by half. Strain the stock through a fine sieve and return it to the cleaned pan.

Bring a large pot of salted water to the boil and add the Chinese broccoli, stalk side down. Cook for 2–3 minutes or until just tender, then drain well and arrange on a serving dish. Just before serving, pour the hot chicken stock mixture over the greens.

Preheat the flat grill plate to medium direct heat. Cook the chicken for 7–8 minutes on each side, or until it is cooked through. Transfer the chicken to a plate, cover it loosely with foil and leave it to rest. When ready to serve, garnish the chicken with coriander sprigs and offer it with the Chinese broccoli and steamed rice.

SERVES 4

Blackened chicken
with crispy tortillas

4 vine-ripened tomatoes, cut
    into 1 cm (½ inch) thick slices
1 teaspoon caster (superfine)
    sugar
1 red onion, sliced
150 ml (5 fl oz) olive oil
1 avocado
3 tablespoons sour cream
100 ml (3½ fl oz) milk
2 tablespoons lime juice

2 x 16 cm (6¼ inch) corn tortillas
1 teaspoon dried oregano
2½ teaspoons ground cumin
1¼ teaspoons garlic salt
½ teaspoon cayenne pepper
4 small boneless, skinless
    chicken breasts
1 large handful coriander
    (cilantro) leaves

Put the tomato slices in a wide dish, sprinkle with sugar and season. Layer the onion over the top and drizzle with 3 tablespoons of the oil. Refrigerate until needed.

Blend the avocado, sour cream, milk, lime juice and 4 tablespoons water in a food processor for 1 minute or until smooth. Season.

Cut each of the tortillas into eight 2 cm (¾ inch) wide strips. Combine the oregano, cumin, garlic salt and cayenne pepper, and coat the chicken breasts in the spice mixture, pressing down firmly with your fingers. Heat 1½ tablespoons of oil over medium–high heat in a large, non-stick frying pan until hot. Cook the chicken for 4 minutes on each side, or until cooked through. Remove from the pan. In the same pan, add 3 tablespoons of oil. Fry the tortilla strips until golden, turning once.

Arrange a small round of tomato and onion slices on four plates. Slice the chicken into 2 cm (¾ inch) thick slices and arrange over the tomato. Drizzle with the avocado dressing and top with four tortilla strips. Sprinkle with coriander and serve.

SERVES 4

Stuffed chicken breast

4 large boneless, skinless chicken breasts
100 g (3½ oz) semi-dried (sun-blushed) tomatoes
100 g (3½ oz) goat's cheese, sliced
200 g (7 oz) asparagus, trimmed, halved and blanched
50 g (1¾ oz) butter
375 ml (13 fl oz/1½ cups) chicken stock
2 zucchini (courgettes), cut into 5 cm (2 inch) batons
250 ml (9 fl oz/1 cup) pouring (whipping) cream
8 spring onions (scallions), thinly sliced

Pound each chicken breast between two sheets of plastic wrap with a mallet or rolling pin until about 1 cm (½ inch) thick. Divide the tomato, goat's cheese and 150 g (5½ oz) of the asparagus pieces among the breasts. Roll up tightly lengthways, securing along the seam with toothpicks.

Heat the butter in a large frying pan over medium heat. Add the chicken, then brown all over. Pour in the stock, then reduce the heat to low. Cook, covered, for 10 minutes, or until the chicken is cooked through. Remove the chicken from the pan and keep warm.

Meanwhile, bring a saucepan of lightly salted water to the boil. Add the zucchini and remaining asparagus and cook for 2 minutes, or until just tender. Remove from the pan. Whisk the cream into the frying pan. Add the spring onion and simmer over medium–low heat for 4 minutes, or until reduced and thickened. To serve, cut each chicken roll in half on the diagonal and place on serving plates. Spoon on the sauce and serve with the greens.

SERVES 4

Zesty chargrilled chicken

3 teaspoons finely grated fresh ginger
2 handfuls coriander (cilantro) leaves, chopped
1½ teaspoons grated lime zest
4 tablespoons lime juice
4 boneless, skinless chicken breasts
2 tablespoons oil
3 zucchini (courgettes), cut into wedges
4 large flat mushrooms, stems trimmed

Combine the ginger, coriander, lime zest and 2 tablespoons of the lime juice in a bowl. Spread 2 teaspoons of the herb mixture over each piece of chicken and season well. Combine the remaining herb mixture with the remaining lime juice in a screwtop jar. Set aside until needed.

Lightly oil a barbecue chargrill plate or flat plate and heat it to medium direct heat. Brush the zucchini and mushrooms with the oil. Place the chicken on the chargrill and cook on each side for 4–5 minutes, or until cooked through. Add the vegetables during the last 5 minutes of cooking, and turn frequently until browned on the outside and just softened. Cover with foil until ready to serve.

Cut the chicken breasts into long thick strips. Shake the dressing well and drizzle over the chicken and serve with the chargrilled vegetables and steamed rice.

SERVES 4

Ginger chicken stir-fry with hokkien noodles

2½ tablespoons finely shredded
    fresh ginger
3 tablespoons mirin
2 tablespoons soy sauce
600 g (1 lb 5 oz) chicken
    tenderloins or boneless,
    skinless chicken breasts, cut
    on the diagonal into thin strips

175 g (6 oz) baby corn
350 g (12 oz) choy sum
150 g (5½ oz) oyster mushrooms
500 g (1 lb 2 oz) hokkien (egg)
    noodles, gently separated
2 tablespoons oil
2 tablespoons oyster sauce

Combine the ginger, mirin and soy sauce in a large non-metallic bowl. Add the chicken and coat it in the marinade. Marinate while your prepare the vegetables.

Cut the corn in half lengthways; trim the ends off the choy sum and cut into 6 cm (2½ inch) lengths. If the mushrooms are very large, cut them in half. Soak the noodles in a large heatproof bowl in boiling water for 5 minutes. Drain and refresh under cold running water.

Heat a wok to very hot, add 1 tablespoon of the oil and swirl to coat the side. Remove the chicken from the marinade with a slotted spoon and cook in two batches over very high heat for 2 minutes, or until brown and just cooked. Remove from the wok.

Add the remaining oil to the wok and stir-fry the mushrooms and corn for 1–2 minutes, or until just softened. Add the remaining marinade, bring to the boil, then add the chicken, choy sum and noodles. Stir in the oyster sauce and cook, tossing well, for 1–2 minutes, or until the choy sum has wilted slightly and the noodles are warmed through. Serve immediately.

SERVES 4

Tandoori chicken with cardamom rice

200 g (7 oz) plain yoghurt, plus
    extra, to serve
3 tablespoons good-quality
    tandoori paste
2 tablespoons lemon juice
1 kg (2 lb 4 oz) boneless, skinless
    chicken breasts, cut into bite-
    sized cubes

1 tablespoon oil
1 onion, finely diced
300 g (10½ oz/1½ cups) long-
    grain rice
2 cardamom pods, bruised
750 ml (26 fl oz/3 cups) hot
    chicken stock
400 g (14 oz) English spinach

Soak eight wooden skewers in water to prevent scorching. Combine the yoghurt, tandoori paste and lemon juice in a non-metallic dish. Add the chicken and coat it in the marinade. Cover and marinate for 10 minutes, or overnight if time permits.

Heat the oil in a saucepan. Add the onion and cook for 3 minutes, then add the rice and cardamom pods. Cook, stirring often, for 3–5 minutes, or until the rice is slightly opaque. Add the stock and bring to the boil. Reduce the heat to low, cover, and cook, without removing the lid, for 15 minutes.

Meanwhile, lightly oil a barbecue flat plate and heat it to high direct heat. Thread the chicken cubes onto the skewers, leaving the bottom quarter of the skewers empty. Cook on each side for 4–5 minutes, or until cooked through.

While the chicken is cooking, wash the spinach and put in a large saucepan with just the water clinging to the leaves. Cook, covered, over medium heat for 1–2 minutes, or until the spinach has wilted. Uncover the rice, fluff with a fork and serve with the spinach, chicken and extra yoghurt.

SERVES 4

Parmesan chicken with piquant green sauce

3 eggs
3 handfuls basil
2 tablespoons capers, rinsed
1 tablespoon dijon mustard
2 tablespoons grated parmesan
  cheese
185 ml (6 fl oz/¾ cup) olive oil

100 g (3½ oz/1 cup) dry
  breadcrumbs
4 small boneless, skinless
  chicken breasts
150 g (5½ oz) rocket (arugula)
  leaves
lemon wedges, to serve

To make the sauce, put 1 egg in a saucepan of cold water, bring to the boil and cook for 1 minute. Remove from the heat and refresh under cold water. Peel, then put in a food processor with the basil, capers, mustard and 1 tablespoon of the parmesan and mix until combined. Gradually add 3 tablespoons of the olive oil and process until you have a coarse sauce, taking care not to overprocess.

Beat the remaining eggs together with 1 tablespoon water. Combine the breadcrumbs with the remaining parmesan on a plate. Pound each chicken breast between two sheets of plastic wrap with a mallet or rolling pin until 5 mm (¼ inch) thick. Dip the chicken in the egg mixture, then coat in the breadcrumb mixture. Place on a paper-lined baking tray and refrigerate for 10 minutes, or until needed.

Heat the remaining oil in a large frying pan over high heat. Cook the chicken in two batches for 2–3 minutes each batch, or until golden on both sides and cooked through — keep each batch warm. Serve with the green sauce, rocket and lemon.

SERVES 4

Sage and ricotta stuffed chicken breast

250 g (9 oz/1 cup) fresh ricotta cheese, well drained
1 tablespoon shredded sage
2 garlic cloves, crushed
1½ teaspoons grated lemon zest
3 tablespoons finely grated parmesan cheese
4 boneless, skinless chicken breasts, tenderloin removed
8 thin slices prosciutto
olive oil, for brushing

Mix together the ricotta, sage, garlic, lemon zest and parmesan until they are well combined. Use a sharp knife to cut a large pocket into the side of each chicken breast and fill each pocket with one-quarter of the ricotta mixture. Pin the pockets closed with toothpicks and wrap each breast in two slices of prosciutto, tightly securing it with a toothpick.

Heat a barbecue flat plate to medium direct heat, brush the chicken parcels with olive oil and season them with freshly ground black pepper. Cook them for 8 minutes on each side, or until cooked through. This is delicious served with a baby spinach salad.

SERVES 4

Chicken pilau

300 g (10½ oz/1½ cups) basmati
  rice
2 tablespoons oil
1 large onion, chopped
3–4 garlic cloves, crushed
1 tablespoon finely chopped
  fresh ginger
500 g (1 lb 2 oz) chicken
  tenderloins, cut into bite-
  sized cubes

300 g (10½ oz) Swiss brown
  mushrooms, sliced
90 g (3¼ oz/¾ cup) slivered
  almonds, toasted
1½–2 teaspoons garam masala,
  dry roasted
125 g (4½ oz/½ cup) plain
  yoghurt
1 tablespoon finely chopped
  coriander (cilantro) leaves,
  plus extra, to garnish

Rinse the rice under cold water until the water runs clear. Drain well. Heat the oil in a large saucepan and stir in the onion, garlic and ginger. Reduce the heat to medium and cook, covered, for 3 minutes, or until the onion has browned. Increase the heat to high, add the chicken and cook, stirring, for 3 minutes, or until the chicken is lightly browned. Stir in the mushrooms, almonds and garam masala. Cook, covered, for another 3 minutes, or until the mushrooms are soft. Uncover and cook without stirring for 2 minutes, or until the liquid has evaporated.

Remove the chicken from the pan. Add the rice and stir for 30 seconds, or until well coated in the mushroom and onion mixture. Pour in 375 ml (13 fl oz/1½ cups) water and bring to the boil. Continue boiling, stirring frequently, for 2 minutes, or until most of the water has evaporated. Return the chicken to the pan. Cover, reduce the heat to low and steam for 15 minutes, or until the rice is cooked.

Combine the yoghurt and chopped coriander. Fluff the rice with a fork, then scoop into bowls. Top with a dollop of the yoghurt mixture and garnish with coriander.

SERVES 4–6

Margarita chicken

3 tablespoons tequila
3 tablespoons lime juice
2 small chillies, finely chopped
3 garlic cloves, crushed
3 tablespoons finely chopped
   coriander (cilantro) leaves
1 tablespoon olive oil
4 boneless chicken breasts (skin on),
   tenderloin removed
lime wedges, to serve

Combine the tequila, lime juice, chilli, garlic, coriander and oil in a large non-metallic bowl. Add the chicken and coat it in the marinade. Cover and marinate for 10 minutes, or overnight if time permits.

Lightly oil a barbecue chargrill plate or flat plate and heat it to medium–high direct heat. Remove the chicken breasts from the marinade, season them with salt and pepper, and cook for 7–8 minutes on each side, or until they are cooked through.

Slice the chicken breasts on the diagonal and serve with lime wedges. This is delicious with avocado and grapefruit salad.

SERVES 4

Grilled chicken with capsicum couscous

185 g (6½ oz/1 cup) instant couscous
1 tablespoon olive oil
1 onion, finely chopped
2 zucchini (courgettes), sliced
½ red or yellow chargrilled capsicum (pepper), chopped
12 semi-dried (sun-blushed) tomatoes, chopped
½ tablespoon grated orange zest
250 ml (9 fl oz/1 cup) orange juice
1 large handful chopped mint
8 chicken thighs or 4 chicken breasts (skin on)
40 g (1½ oz) butter, softened

Preheat the grill (broiler). Bring 500 ml (17 fl oz/2 cups) water to the boil in a saucepan, add the couscous, then take the pan off the heat, cover with a lid and leave to stand for 10 minutes.

Heat the oil in a frying pan and fry the onion and zucchini until lightly browned. Add the capsicum and semi-dried tomatoes, then stir in the couscous. Stir in the orange zest, one-third of the orange juice and the mint.

Put the chicken in a large shallow ovenproof dish in a single layer and dot it with the butter. Sprinkle with the remaining orange juice and season well with salt and pepper. Grill the chicken for 8–10 minutes, turning it over halfway through. The skin should be browned and crisp.

Serve the chicken on the couscous with any juices poured over it.

SERVES 4

Stir-fried chicken with capsicum and snow peas

1½ tablespoons vegetable oil
8 spring onions (scallions), cut into short lengths
3 garlic cloves, crushed
8 cm (3¼ inch) piece fresh ginger, finely shredded
2 boneless, skinless chicken breasts, cut into strips
2 red capsicums (peppers), cut into strips
150 g (5½ oz) snow peas (mangetout)
100 g (3½ oz/⅔ cup) cashew nuts
2 tablespoons soy sauce
1½ teaspoons sesame oil

Heat a wok to very hot, add the vegetable oil and swirl to coat the side until it is smoking — this will only take a few seconds. Add the spring onion, garlic and ginger and stir them around for a few seconds. Next, add the chicken and stir it around until it has turned white. Add the capsicum and keep stirring, then throw in the snow peas and cashews and stir-fry for 1–2 minutes.

Once the capsicum has started to soften a little, add the soy sauce and sesame oil, toss everything together, then serve with steamed rice.

SERVES 4

Bacon-wrapped
chicken breasts

2 tablespoons olive oil
2 tablespoons lime juice
¼ teaspoon ground coriander
6 boneless, skinless chicken breasts
4 tablespoons fruit chutney
3 tablespoons chopped pecan nuts
6 bacon slices

Mix together the oil, lime juice, coriander and salt and pepper. Using a sharp knife, cut a pocket in the thickest section of each chicken breast. Mix together the chutney and nuts. Spoon 1 tablespoon of the chutney mixture into each chicken breast pocket.

Turn the tapered ends of the chicken to the underside. Wrap a slice of bacon around each piece to enclose the filling and secure with a toothpick.

Lightly oil a barbecue chargrill plate or flat plate and heat it to high direct heat. Cook the chicken parcels for 5 minutes on each side, or until cooked through, turning once. Brush with the lime juice mixture several times during cooking and drizzle with any leftover lime juice mixture to serve.

SERVES 6

NOTE: This recipe also works well with prosciutto.

Sichuan chicken

¼ teaspoon Chinese five-spice
750 g (1 lb 10 oz) boneless, skinless chicken
   thighs, halved
2 tablespoons oil
1 tablespoon julienned fresh ginger
1 teaspoon Sichuan peppercorns, crushed
1 teaspoon chilli bean paste (toban jian)
2 tablespoons light soy sauce
1 tablespoon Chinese rice wine
600 g (1 lb 5 oz) baby bok choy (pak choy),
   leaves separated

Sprinkle the five-spice over the chicken. Heat a wok to very hot, add half the oil and swirl to coat the side. Add the chicken and cook for 2 minutes on each side, or until browned. Remove from the pan or wok.

Reduce the heat to medium and cook the ginger for 30 seconds. Add the peppercorns and chilli bean paste. Return the chicken to the wok, add the soy sauce, wine and 125 ml (4 fl oz/½ cup) water, then simmer for 15–20 minutes, or until cooked.

Just before the chicken is ready, heat the remaining oil in a saucepan. Add the bok choy and toss for 1 minute, or until the leaves wilt and the stems are tender. Serve with the chicken and some steamed rice.

SERVES 4

Chicken with Thai basil, chilli and cashews

750 g (1 lb 10 oz) boneless, skinless chicken breasts or thighs, cut into strips
2 lemongrass stems, white part only, finely chopped
3 small red chillies, seeded and finely chopped
4 garlic cloves, crushed
1 tablespoon finely chopped fresh ginger
2 coriander roots, finely chopped
2 tablespoons oil
100 g (3½ oz/⅔ cup) cashew nuts
1½ tablespoons lime juice
2 tablespoons fish sauce
1½ tablespoons grated palm sugar (jaggery) or soft brown sugar
60 g (2¼ oz/2 cups) Thai basil
2 teaspoons cornflour (cornstarch) mixed with 1 tablespoon water

Put the chicken in a large bowl with the lemongrass, chilli, garlic, ginger and coriander root. Mix together well.

Heat a wok to medium, add 1 teaspoon of the oil and swirl to coat the side. Add the cashews and cook for 1 minute, or until lightly golden. Remove and drain on crumpled paper towels.

Heat the remaining oil in the wok, add the chicken in batches and stir-fry over medium heat for 4–5 minutes, or until browned. Return the chicken to the wok.

Stir in the lime juice, fish sauce, sugar and basil, and cook for 30–60 seconds, or until the basil just begins to wilt. Add the cornflour mixture and stir until the mixture thickens slightly. Stir in the cashews and serve with steamed rice.

SERVES 4

Chargrilled chicken
with salsa verde

1 garlic clove
60 g (2¼ oz) flat-leaf (Italian) parsley
4 tablespoons extra virgin olive oil
3 tablespoons chopped dill
1½ tablespoons dijon mustard
1 tablespoon sherry vinegar
1 tablespoon baby capers, drained
6 large boneless, skinless chicken breasts

Put the garlic, parsley, oil, dill, mustard, vinegar and capers in a food processor
or blender and process until almost smooth.

Lightly oil a barbecue chargrill plate or flat plate and heat it to high direct heat.
Cook the chicken breasts for 4–5 minutes on each side, or until cooked through.

Cut each chicken breast into three on the diagonal and arrange on serving plates.
Top with a spoonful of salsa verde and season to taste.

SERVES 6

Teriyaki chicken with ginger chive rice

4 small boneless chicken breasts,
  skin on
3 tablespoons Japanese soy sauce
2 tablespoons sake
1½ tablespoons mirin
1½ tablespoons soft brown
  sugar

3 teaspoons finely grated
  fresh ginger
300 g (10½ oz/1½ cups)
  long-grain rice
2 tablespoons finely snipped
  chives
2 tablespoons oil

Pound each breast between two sheets of plastic wrap with a mallet or rolling pin until 1 cm (½ inch) thick. Put the soy sauce, sake, mirin, sugar and 1 teaspoon of the ginger in a flat non-metallic dish and stir until the sugar has dissolved. Add the chicken and coat in the marinade. Cover and marinate for 10 minutes.

Bring a large saucepan of water to the boil. Add the rice and cook for 12 minutes, stirring occasionally. Drain. Stir in the chives and remaining ginger, then cover until ready to serve.

Meanwhile, drain the chicken, reserving the marinade. Heat the oil in a deep frying pan and cook the chicken, skin side down, over medium heat for 5 minutes, until the skin is crisp. Turn and cook for a further 4 minutes (not quite cooked). Remove from the pan and allow to rest.

Add the marinade and 3 tablespoons water to the frying pan and scrape up any sediment. Bring to the boil over high heat, then add the chicken, skin side up, and any resting juices. Cook for about 5 minutes, until the chicken is cooked through and the sauce is syrupy. Serve the chicken on a bed of rice, drizzled with the sauce.

SERVES 4

Tagliatelle with chicken, herbs and mushrooms

2 tablespoons olive oil
350 g (12 oz) chicken tenderloins,
 cut into bite-sized cubes
20 g (¾ oz) butter
400 g (14 oz) mushrooms, sliced
2 garlic cloves, finely chopped
125 ml (4 fl oz/½ cup) dry white
 wine
185 ml (6 fl oz/¾ cup) pouring
 (whipping) cream

400 g (14 oz) tagliatelle
1 teaspoon finely grated
 lemon zest
2 tablespoons lemon juice
2 tablespoons chopped
 marjoram
2 tablespoons chopped parsley
100 g (3½ oz/1 cup) grated
 parmesan cheese

Heat 1 tablespoon of the oil in a large frying pan, add the chicken and cook over medium heat for 3–4 minutes, or until lightly browned. Remove from the pan.

Heat the butter and remaining oil in the pan, add the mushrooms and cook, stirring, over high heat for 3 minutes. Add the garlic and cook for another 2 minutes.

Stir in the wine, reduce the heat and simmer for 5 minutes, or until it has almost evaporated. Stir in the cream and chicken, and simmer for 5 minutes, or until the sauce has thickened.

Meanwhile, bring a large saucepan of salted water to the boil and cook the pasta according to the packet instructions until *al dente*. Drain and keep warm.

Stir the lemon zest and juice, marjoram, parsley and 2 tablespoons of the parmesan into the sauce. Season, combine with the pasta and serve with the remaining parmesan.

SERVES 4

Thai green chicken curry with coriander rice

250 g (9 oz/1¼ cups) jasmine rice
1 tablespoon oil
1–2 tablespoons Thai green curry paste
4 makrut (kaffir lime) leaves
1 tablespoon fish sauce
2 teaspoons grated palm sugar (jaggery) or soft brown sugar
400 ml (14 fl oz) tin coconut cream
750 g (1 lb 10 oz) boneless, skinless chicken breasts, cut into strips
4 tablespoons roughly chopped coriander (cilantro) leaves
2 tablespoons whole coriander (cilantro) leaves

Bring a large saucepan of water to the boil. Add the rice and cook for 12 minutes, stirring occasionally. Drain well.

Meanwhile, heat the oil over high heat in a saucepan or wok, then add the curry paste and lime leaves and fry over medium–high heat for 1–2 minutes, or until fragrant. Add the fish sauce and sugar and mix well. Pour in the coconut cream, bring to the boil, then add the chicken strips. Reduce the heat to medium and simmer for 12–15 minutes, or until the sauce is reduced and the chicken is tender and cooked.

Just before serving, stir the chopped coriander through the rice. Serve the curry over the coriander rice, garnished with the whole coriander leaves.

SERVES 4

Chicken, snake bean and Thai basil stir-fry

3 tablespoons oil
500 g (1 lb 2 oz) boneless, skinless chicken breasts,
    cut into thin strips
1 garlic clove, crushed
4 spring onions (scallions), thinly sliced
150 g (5½ oz) snake (yard-long) beans,
    trimmed and cut into 5 cm (2 inch) lengths
2 small red chillies, thinly sliced
3 handfuls Thai basil, plus extra, to garnish
2 tablespoons chopped mint
1 tablespoon fish sauce
1 tablespoon oyster sauce
2 teaspoons lime juice
1 tablespoon grated palm sugar (jaggery)
    or soft brown sugar

Heat a wok to high, add 1 tablespoon of the oil and swirl to coat the side. Cook the chicken in batches for 3–5 minutes, or until lightly browned and almost cooked — add more oil if needed. Remove and keep warm.

Heat the remaining oil in the wok. Add the garlic, onion, snake beans and chilli, and stir-fry for 1 minute, or until the onion is tender. Add the chicken to the wok.

Toss in the basil and mint, then add the combined fish sauce, oyster sauce, lime juice, sugar and 2 tablespoons water and cook for 1 minute. Garnish with the extra basil and serve with jasmine rice.

SERVES 4

Hot and sweet chicken

125 ml (4 fl oz/½ cup) rice
   vinegar
165 g (5¾ oz) caster (superfine)
   sugar
6 garlic cloves, crushed
large pinch chilli flakes
1 teaspoon ground coriander
1 teaspoon ground white pepper
175 g (6 oz) coriander (cilantro),
   finely chopped, including
   roots and stems

3 tablespoons oil
2 tablespoons lemon juice
8 boneless, skinless chicken
   thighs, halved
2 tablespoons caster (superfine)
   sugar, extra
2 tablespoons fish sauce
1 Lebanese (short) cucumber,
   peeled and sliced

To make the sauce, combine the vinegar and sugar in a small saucepan, bring to the boil, then turn down the heat and simmer for 1 minute. Take the mixture off the heat and add 2 of the crushed garlic cloves, the chilli flakes and a pinch of salt. Leave the sauce to cool.

Heat a small frying pan for 1 minute, add the ground coriander and white pepper and stir constantly for 1 minute. Add the rest of the garlic, the fresh coriander and a pinch of salt. Add 2 tablespoons of the oil and all the lemon juice and mix to a paste. Rub this all over the chicken pieces.

Heat the rest of the oil in a wok, add the chicken and fry it on both sides for 8 minutes, or until it is cooked through. Sprinkle in the extra sugar and the fish sauce and cook for another 1–2 minutes, or until any excess liquid has evaporated and the chicken pieces are sticky. Serve the chicken with the sliced cucumber and some rice. Drizzle with the sauce.

SERVES 4

Chicken, baby corn and bok choy stir-fry

1 tablespoon cornflour
  (cornstarch)
2 teaspoons finely chopped
  fresh ginger
2 garlic cloves, crushed
1 small red chilli, finely chopped
1 teaspoon sesame oil
3 tablespoons light soy sauce
500 g (1 lb 2 oz) boneless, skinless
  chicken breasts, thinly sliced

1 tablespoon vegetable oil
1 onion, halved and thinly sliced
115 g (4 oz) baby corn, halved
  on the diagonal
425 g (15 oz) baby bok choy
  (pak choy), trimmed and
  quartered lengthways
2 tablespoons oyster sauce
3 tablespoons chicken stock

Combine half the cornflour with the ginger, crushed garlic, chilli, sesame oil and 2 tablespoons soy sauce in a large bowl. Add the chicken, toss until well coated and marinate for 10 minutes, or overnight if time permits.

Heat a wok to hot, add the vegetable oil and swirl to coat the side. Stir-fry the onion for 2 minutes, or until soft and golden. Add the chicken in two batches and stir-fry each batch for 5 minutes, or until almost cooked through, then remove from the wok. Add the baby corn and stir-fry for a further 2 minutes, then add the bok choy and cook for 2 minutes, or until wilted. Return all the chicken to the wok.

Mix the remaining soy sauce and cornflour with the oyster sauce and chicken stock in a small bowl, add to the wok and stir-fry for 1–2 minutes, or until the sauce has thickened to a coating consistency and the chicken is cooked. Serve immediately with steamed rice.

SERVES 4

Chicken breasts with mustard cream sauce

4 boneless, skinless chicken breasts
2 tablespoons olive oil
1 garlic clove, crushed
3 tablespoons dry white wine
2 tablespoons wholegrain mustard
2 teaspoons chopped thyme
300 ml (10½ fl oz) pouring (whipping) cream

Pound each chicken breast between two sheets of plastic wrap with a mallet or rolling pin until about 1 cm (½ inch) thick.

Heat the oil in a frying pan over high heat. Brown the chicken breasts for 4–5 minutes on each side, or until brown. Remove and cover with foil.

Add the garlic to the frying pan and cook for 1 minute over medium heat, then stir in the wine, mustard and thyme. Increase the heat to medium–high and pour in the cream. Simmer for about 5 minutes, or until the sauce has reduced and thickened slightly, then season to taste.

Serve the chicken with a drizzle of sauce and some steamed vegetables.

SERVES 4

Stracci with artichokes and chargrilled chicken

3 boneless, skinless chicken breasts
500 g (1 lb 2 oz) stracci pasta
8 slices prosciutto
280 g (10 oz) jar artichokes in oil, drained
  and quartered, oil reserved
150 g (5½ oz) semi-dried (sun-blushed)
  tomatoes, thinly sliced
80 g (2¾ oz) baby rocket (arugula) leaves
2–3 tablespoons balsamic vinegar

Lightly brush a chargrill or frying pan with oil and heat over high heat. Cook the chicken for 6–8 minutes on each side, or until cooked through. Cut into thin slices on the diagonal. Preheat the grill (broiler).

Bring a large saucepan of salted water to the boil and cook the pasta according to the packet instructions until *al dente*.

Meanwhile, put the prosciutto on a lined grill tray and grill for 2 minutes on each side, or until crisp. Cool slightly and break into pieces. Drain the pasta, then combine with the chicken, prosciutto, artichokes, tomato and rocket in a bowl and toss. Whisk together 3 tablespoons of the reserved artichoke oil and the balsamic vinegar and toss through the pasta mixture. Season to taste with salt and freshly ground black pepper, then serve.

SERVES 6

Mirin and sake chicken

2 tablespoons mirin
2 tablespoons sake
1 tablespoon oil
4 large boneless, skinless chicken breasts
5 cm (2 inch) piece fresh ginger, very thinly sliced
3 teaspoons soy sauce

Combine the mirin, sake and oil in a large non-metallic dish. Add the chicken and coat in the marinade. Cover and marinate for 15 minutes, then drain the chicken, reserving the marinade.

Lightly oil a barbecue chargrill plate or flat plate and heat it to high direct heat. Cook the chicken for 4 minutes on each side, or until tender.

Put the ginger in a pan and add the reserved marinade. Boil for about 7 minutes, or until thickened. Drizzle the soy sauce over the chicken and top with the ginger. Serve immediately on a bed of salad leaves.

SERVES 4

Satay chicken stir-fry

1½ tablespoons oil
6 spring onions (scallions), cut into 3 cm (1¼ inch) lengths
800 g (1 lb 12 oz) boneless, skinless chicken breasts,
   thinly sliced on the diagonal
1–1½ tablespoons Thai red curry paste
4 tablespoons crunchy peanut butter
270 ml (9½ fl oz) coconut milk
2 teaspoons soft brown sugar
1½ tablespoons lime juice

Heat a wok to very hot, add 1 teaspoon of the oil and swirl to coat the side. When hot, add the spring onion and stir-fry for 30 seconds, or until softened slightly. Remove from the wok. Add a little extra oil to the wok as needed and stir-fry the chicken in three batches for about 1 minute per batch, or until the meat just changes colour. Remove from the wok.

Add a little more oil to the wok, add the curry paste and stir-fry for 1 minute, or until fragrant. Add the peanut butter, coconut milk, sugar and 250 ml (9 fl oz/1 cup) water and stir well. Bring to the boil and boil for 3–4 minutes, or until thickened and the oil starts to separate — reduce the heat slightly if the sauce spits at you. Return the chicken and the spring onion to the wok, stir well and cook for 2 minutes, or until heated through. Stir in the lime juice and season. Serve at once with steamed rice and a crisp green salad.

SERVES 4

slow

Chicken with cashews and home-made chilli jam

Chilli jam

10 dried long red chillies

4 tablespoons oil

1 red capsicum (pepper), chopped

1 garlic bulb, peeled and roughly chopped

200 g (7 oz) red Asian shallots, chopped

100 g (3½ oz) grated palm sugar (jaggery) or soft brown sugar

2 tablespoons tamarind purée (see Note)

1 tablespoon oil

6 spring onions (scallions), cut into 3 cm (1¼ inch) lengths

500 g (1 lb 2 oz) boneless, skinless chicken breasts, sliced

4 tablespoons cashew nuts, toasted

1 tablespoon fish sauce

1 handful Thai basil

To make the chilli jam, soak the chillies in a bowl of boiling water for 15 minutes. Drain, remove the seeds and chop. Put in a food processor, then add the oil, capsicum, garlic and shallots and blend until smooth.

Heat a wok to medium heat and add the chilli mixture. Cook, stirring occasionally, for 15 minutes. Add the sugar and tamarind and simmer for 10 minutes, or until it darkens and reaches a jam-like consistency. Remove from the wok.

Clean and reheat the wok over high heat, add the oil and swirl to coat. Stir-fry the spring onion for 1 minute, then add the chicken and stir-fry for 3–5 minutes, or until golden and tender. Stir in the cashews, fish sauce and 4 tablespoons of the chilli jam. Stir-fry for a further 2 minutes, then stir in the basil and serve with rice.

SERVES 4

NOTE: Use a non-stick or stainless steel wok to cook this recipe because the tamarind purée will react with the metal in a regular wok and will taint the dish.

Five-spice roast chicken

1.8 kg (4 lb) whole chicken
1 tablespoon soy sauce
2 garlic cloves, crushed
1 teaspoon finely grated fresh ginger
1 tablespoon honey
1 tablespoon Chinese rice wine
1 teaspoon five-spice
1 tablespoon oil

Wash the chicken and thoroughly pat it dry inside and out with paper towels. Whisk the soy sauce, garlic, ginger, honey, rice wine and five-spice together in a small bowl and brush it all over the chicken, ensuring every bit of skin is well coated. Put the chicken on a wire rack over a baking tray and refrigerate it, uncovered, for at least 8 hours, or overnight if time permits.

Preheat a kettle or covered barbecue to medium indirect heat and put a drip tray under the rack. Brush the chicken liberally with the oil and put it, breast side up, in the middle of the barbecue over the drip tray. Cover the barbecue and roast the chicken for 1 hour 10 minutes, or until the juices run clear when you pierce it with a skewer between the thigh and body. Check the chicken every so often, and if it appears to be over-browning, cover it loosely with foil. Leave it to rest, covered, for 10 minutes before carving and serving with steamed Asian greens and rice.

SERVES 4

Chicken and asparagus risotto

1.5 litres (52 fl oz/6 cups) chicken stock
250 ml (9 fl oz/1 cup) dry white wine
6 whole black peppercorns
2 bay leaves
1 tablespoon olive oil
40 g (1½ oz) butter
600 g (1 lb 5 oz) boneless, skinless chicken breasts, cut into bite-sized cubes
1 leek, white part only, sliced
2 garlic cloves, crushed
440 g (15½ oz/2 cups) risotto rice
200 g (7 oz) asparagus, trimmed and cut into 3 cm (1¼ inch) lengths
50 g (1¾ oz/½ cup) grated parmesan cheese
2 tablespoons lemon juice
3 tablespoons chopped parsley
shaved parmesan cheese, to garnish

Put the stock, wine, peppercorns and bay leaves in a saucepan and simmer for 5 minutes. Strain through a sieve, return to the cleaned pan and keep at a low simmer.

Heat the oil and half the butter in a saucepan, add the chicken and cook over medium heat for 5 minutes, or until golden. Remove. Add the leek and garlic and cook for 5 minutes, or until softened.

Add the rice and stir for 1 minute to coat the grains. Add 125 ml (4 fl oz/½ cup) stock, stirring until it has been absorbed. Continue adding stock, 125 ml (4 fl oz/½ cup) at a time, stirring constantly for 20–25 minutes, until the stock is absorbed and the rice is tender. Add the asparagus and chicken in the last 5 minutes.

When the chicken is cooked through, stir in the parmesan, juice, parsley and remaining butter. Season, and garnish with the shaved parmesan before serving.

SERVES 4

Chicken casserole with olives and tomatoes

1 tablespoon olive oil
1 large onion, chopped
2 garlic cloves, crushed
8 chicken pieces on the bone (skin on)
1 tablespoon tomato paste (concentrated purée)
375 ml (13 fl oz/1½ cups) dry white wine
pinch sugar
8 large ripe tomatoes, chopped
4 tablespoons flat-leaf (Italian) parsley, chopped
180 g (6½ oz) green beans, trimmed and halved
130 g (4½ oz) black olives

Heat the oil in a large flameproof casserole and fry the onion for 1–2 minutes. Add the garlic and the chicken and fry for as long as it takes to brown the chicken all over.

Add the tomato paste and white wine, along with the sugar, and stir everything together. Add the tomato and any juices, the parsley and the beans and bring to the boil. Turn down the heat, season well and simmer for 40 minutes.

Add the olives and simmer for another 5 minutes. The sauce should be thick by now and the chicken fully cooked. Add more salt and pepper, if necessary. Serve with potatoes, pasta or rice.

SERVES 4

Butter chicken

2 tablespoons oil
1 kg (2 lb 4 oz) boneless, skinless
  chicken thighs, quartered
60 g (2¼ oz) butter or ghee
2 teaspoons garam masala
2 teaspoons sweet paprika
2 teaspoons ground coriander
1 tablespoon finely chopped
  fresh ginger

¼ teaspoon chilli powder
1 cinnamon stick
6 cardamom pods, bruised
350 g (12 oz) puréed tomatoes
1 tablespoon sugar
3 tablespoons plain yoghurt
125 ml (4 fl oz/½ cup) pouring
  (whipping) cream
1 tablespoon lemon juice

Heat a wok to very hot, add 1 tablespoon of the oil and swirl to coat the side. Add half the boneless, skinless chicken thighs and stir-fry for 4 minutes, or until browned. Remove. Add extra oil, as needed, and cook the remaining chicken. Remove.

Reduce the heat, add the butter to the wok and melt. Add the garam masala, sweet paprika, coriander, ginger, chilli powder, cinnamon stick and cardamom pods, and stir-fry for 1 minute, or until fragrant. Return the chicken to the wok and mix to coat in the spices.

Add the tomato and sugar, and simmer, stirring, for 15 minutes, or until the chicken is tender and the sauce has thickened.

Add the yoghurt, cream and juice and simmer for 5 minutes, or until the sauce has thickened slightly. Serve with rice and pappadums.

SERVES 4–6

Sausage and white bean stew

2 tablespoons olive oil
8 chicken sausages, cut into 4 cm (1½ inch) lengths
1 leek, white part only, thinly sliced
1 red capsicum (pepper), chopped
400 g (14 oz) tin chopped tomatoes
125 ml (4 fl oz/½ cup) chicken stock
300 g (10½ oz) tin butter beans, drained and rinsed
2 tablespoons flat-leaf (Italian) parsley

Heat half the oil in a saucepan over medium heat, add the sausage and cook for 6 minutes, or until browned. Remove from the pan.

Heat the remaining oil in the pan, add the leek and cook over low heat for about 10 minutes, or until softened. Add the capsicum and cook for a further 2 minutes. Return the sausage to the pan and stir in the tomato and stock.

Bring to the boil, then reduce the heat and simmer for 30 minutes. Add the beans, season and stir for 1–2 minutes to heat through. Garnish with the parsley and serve with couscous.

SERVES 4

Chicken braised with ginger and star anise

1 teaspoon Sichuan peppercorns
2 tablespoons oil
2 x 3 cm (¾ x 1¼ inch) piece fresh ginger, julienned
2 garlic cloves, chopped
1 kg (2 lb 4 oz) boneless, skinless chicken thighs, halved
4 tablespoons Chinese rice wine
1 tablespoon honey
3 tablespoons light soy sauce
1 star anise

Heat a wok to medium, add the peppercorns and cook, stirring to prevent burning, for 2–4 minutes, or until fragrant. Remove and lightly crush with the back of a knife.

Reheat the wok, add the oil and swirl to coat. Add the ginger and garlic and cook over low heat for 1–2 minutes, or until slightly golden. Increase the heat to medium, add the chicken in batches and cook for 3 minutes, or until browned all over. Return all the chicken to the wok.

Add the peppercorns, wine, honey, soy sauce and star anise to the wok, reduce the heat to low and simmer, covered, for 20 minutes, or until the chicken is tender. Divide among four bowls and serve with steamed rice.

SERVES 4

Spanish saffron chicken and rice

3 tablespoons olive oil
4 chicken thighs on the bone and 6 drumsticks (skin on)
1 large red onion, finely chopped
1 large green capsicum (pepper), two-thirds diced
    and one-third julienned
3 teaspoons sweet paprika
400 g (14 oz) tin diced tomatoes
275 g (9¾ oz/1¼ cups) paella or risotto rice
½ teaspoon ground saffron

Heat 2 tablespoons of the oil in a large deep frying pan over high heat. Season the chicken pieces well and brown in batches. Remove the chicken from the pan.

Reduce the pan to medium heat and add the remaining oil. Add the onion and the diced capsicum and cook gently for 5 minutes. Stir in the paprika and cook for 30 seconds. Add the tomato and simmer for 1–3 minutes, or until it thickens.

Stir 875 ml (30 fl oz/3½ cups) boiling water into the pan, then add the rice and saffron. Return the chicken to the pan and stir to combine. Season with salt and pepper. Bring to the boil, then cover, reduce the heat to medium–low and simmer for 20–30 minutes, or until all the liquid has been absorbed and the chicken is tender. Stir the julienned capsicum into the pan, then allow to stand, covered, for a few minutes before serving.

SERVES 4

Chicken fricassée

25 g (1 oz) butter
1 tablespoon olive oil
200 g (7 oz) button mushrooms, sliced
1.5 kg (3 lb 5 oz) chicken pieces on the bone (skin on)
1 onion, chopped
2 celery stalks, sliced
250 ml (9 fl oz/1 cup) dry white wine
250 ml (9 fl oz/1 cup) chicken stock
1 bay leaf
250 ml (9 fl oz/1 cup) pouring (whipping) cream
2 tablespoons chopped parsley

Heat half the butter and oil in a large saucepan. Add the mushrooms and cook over medium heat for 5 minutes, or until soft and golden. Remove from the pan with a slotted spoon. Heat the remaining oil and butter, add the chicken pieces in batches and cook for 4 minutes, or until browned. Remove from the pan.

Add the onion and celery to the pan, and cook for 8 minutes, or until soft. Pour in the wine and stir well. Add the stock, chicken, mushrooms, bay leaf and cream. Bring to the boil, then reduce the heat and simmer, covered, for 30–45 minutes, or until the chicken is cooked through and tender.

Remove the bay leaf, add the chopped parsley and season with salt and freshly ground black pepper. Serve with mashed potato.

SERVES 4

Pasta with roast chicken, pine nuts and lemon

1.3 kg (3 lb) whole chicken
1 garlic bulb, cloves separated
   and left unpeeled
3 tablespoons olive oil
30 g (1 oz) butter, softened
1 tablespoon finely chopped
   thyme
125 ml (4 fl oz/½ cup) lemon juice

500 g (1 lb 2 oz) bavette or
   spaghetti
2 tablespoons currants
1 teaspoon finely grated
   lemon zest
4 tablespoons pine nuts, toasted
1 large handful flat-leaf (Italian)
   parsley, finely chopped

Preheat the oven to 200°C (400°F/Gas 6). Remove the neck from the inside of the chicken and put the neck in a roasting tin. Rinse the inside of the chicken. Insert the garlic cloves into the cavity, then put the chicken into the roasting tin.

Combine the oil, butter, thyme and lemon juice, then rub over the chicken. Season. Roast for 1 hour, or until the skin is golden and the juices run clear when the thigh is pierced with a skewer. Transfer to a bowl to catch any juices while resting. Remove the garlic from the cavity, cool, then squeeze the cloves out of their skins and chop.

Bring a large saucepan of salted water to the boil and cook the pasta according to the packet instructions until *al dente*. Drain and keep warm.

Meanwhile, to make the sauce, pour the juices from the roasting tin into a small saucepan and discard the neck. Add the currants, lemon zest and chopped garlic, then simmer over low heat. Remove all the meat from the chicken and shred into bite-sized pieces. Add the resting juices to the pan with the sauce.

Add the chicken, pine nuts, parsley and sauce to the pasta, toss well and serve.

SERVES 4–6

Sri Lankan chicken curry with cashews

Curry powder
3 tablespoons coriander seeds
1½ tablespoons cumin seeds
1 teaspoon fennel seeds
¼ teaspoon fenugreek seeds
2 cm (¾ inch) cinnamon stick
6 cloves
¼ teaspoon cardamom seeds
2 teaspoons dried curry leaves
2 small dried red chillies
2 tablespoons oil

1 kg (2 lb 4 oz) boneless, skinless
    chicken thighs, halved
1 onion, chopped
2 garlic cloves, crushed
2 teaspoons grated fresh ginger
1 teaspoon ground turmeric
2 x 400 g (14 oz) tins whole
    peeled tomatoes
160 ml (5¼ fl oz) coconut milk
80 g (2¾ oz/½ cup) cashew
    nuts, toasted

Dry-fry the coriander, cumin, fennel and fenugreek seeds until fragrant and browned. Transfer to a small food processor or mortar and pestle, add the remaining curry powder ingredients and process or grind to a powder.

Heat the oil in a large frying pan. Cook the chicken in batches for 10 minutes, or until browned all over. Remove and drain on crumpled paper towels. Drain all but 1 tablespoon of oil from the pan. Add the onion, garlic, ginger and turmeric, and cook for 10 minutes, or until the onion is soft. Add 2 tablespoons of the curry powder and cook, stirring, for 3 minutes, or until fragrant.

Add the tomato and some salt, bring to the boil, then reduce to a simmer. Return the chicken to the pan and stir. Simmer, covered, for 15 minutes, then uncovered for 15 minutes, or until the chicken is tender and the sauce has thickened. Stir in the coconut milk and simmer for 3 minutes. Garnish with cashews and serve with rice.

SERVES 6

Mexican chicken bake

165 g (5¾ oz/¾ cup) short-grain rice
300 g (10½ oz) tin red kidney beans, drained and rinsed
3½ tablespoons chopped coriander (cilantro) leaves
1 tablespoon oil
600 g (1 lb 5 oz) boneless, skinless chicken thighs, unrolled
2 x 200 g (7 oz) jars spicy taco sauce
250 g (9 oz/2 cups) grated cheddar cheese
125 g (4½ oz/½ cup) sour cream

Preheat the oven to 180°C (350°F/Gas 4). Lightly grease a deep (7 cm/2¾ inch) round (21 cm/8¼ inch) ceramic casserole dish. Bring a large saucepan of water to the boil, add the rice and cook for 10–12 minutes, stirring occasionally. Drain.

In the prepared dish, combine the beans and 1½ tablespoons of the coriander, then add the rice and toss together. Lightly press the mixture so the beans are mixed into the rice and the mixture is flat.

Heat the oil in a large frying pan over medium–high heat. Sauté the chicken thighs for 3 minutes, then turn over. Add the spicy taco sauce, and cook for another 3 minutes.

To assemble, spread half the cheese over the rice. Arrange the thighs and sauce on top in a star shape, sprinkle with 1½ tablespoons coriander, then sprinkle with cheese. Cover with foil.

Bake for 35–40 minutes, or until the mixture is bubbling and the cheese is melted and slightly browned — remove the foil for the last 5 minutes. Cut into four servings with a knife and scoop out carefully, keeping the layers intact. Serve sprinkled with the remaining coriander and a dollop of sour cream.

SERVES 4

Chicken curry
with apricots

18 dried apricots
1 tablespoon ghee
2 x 1.5 kg (3 lb 5 oz) whole
   chickens, jointed
3 onions, thinly sliced
1 teaspoon grated fresh
   ginger
3 garlic cloves, crushed

3 large fresh green chillies,
   seeded and finely chopped
1 teaspoon cumin seeds
1 teaspoon chilli powder
½ teaspoon ground turmeric
4 cardamom pods, bruised
4 large tomatoes, peeled and
   cut into eighths

Soak the dried apricots in 250 ml (9 fl oz/1 cup) hot water for 1 hour.

Melt the ghee in a large saucepan, add the chicken in batches and cook over high heat for 5–6 minutes, or until browned. Remove from the pan.

Add the onion to the pan and cook, stirring often, for 10 minutes, or until soft and golden. Add the ginger, garlic and fresh chilli and cook, stirring, for 2 minutes. Stir in the cumin, chilli powder and ground turmeric and cook for a further 1 minute.

Return the chicken to the pan, add the cardamom, tomato and apricots, with any remaining liquid, and mix well. Simmer, covered, for 35 minutes, or until the chicken is tender.

Remove the chicken, cover and keep warm. Bring the liquid to the boil and boil rapidly, uncovered, for 5 minutes, or until it has thickened slightly. Spoon the liquid over the chicken and serve with steamed rice mixed with raisins, grated carrot and toasted flaked almonds.

SERVES 6–8

Roast chicken pieces with herbed cheese

150 g (5½ oz) herbed cream cheese
1 teaspoon grated lemon zest
4 chicken leg quarters or breasts on the bone (skin on)
2 leeks, white part only, cut into chunks
2 parsnips, cut into chunks
2 teaspoons olive oil

Preheat the oven to 200°C (400°F/Gas 6). Mix the cream cheese with the lemon zest. Loosen the skin from the whole legs or chicken breasts and spread 2 tablespoons of the cream cheese between the skin and flesh on each. Press the skin back down and season it with salt and pepper.

Bring a saucepan of water to the boil and cook the leek and parsnip for 4 minutes. Drain them well and put them in a single layer in an ovenproof dish. Drizzle with the oil and season well. Put the chicken on top and put the dish in the oven.

Roast for 40 minutes, by which time the skin should be browned and the cream cheese should have mostly melted out to form a sauce over the vegetables. Check that the vegetables are cooked and tender by prodding them with a knife. If they need a little longer, cover the dish with foil and cook for another 5 minutes. Keep the chicken warm under foil in the meantime. Serve immediately.

SERVES 4

Barbecued whole chicken with zucchini

1.8 kg (4 lb) whole chicken
12 garlic cloves, unpeeled
10 sprigs lemon thyme
1 lemon, halved
1 tablespoon olive oil

8 small zucchini (courgettes),
   halved lengthways
2 tablespoons chopped flat-leaf
   (Italian) parsley

Remove the giblets and any large fat deposits from inside the chicken, then pat it dry inside and out with paper towels. Season the cavity with salt and pepper and stuff it with the unpeeled garlic cloves and the sprigs of thyme. Rub the skin with the cut lemon, making sure that it is evenly coated all over, then brush it with 2 teaspoons of the oil and season with salt and black pepper. Tie the legs together.

Preheat a kettle or covered barbecue to medium indirect heat, with a drip tray underneath the grill. Position the chicken on the barbecue directly over the drip tray, close the hood and roast the chicken for 1 hour, or until the juices run clear when it is pierced with a skewer between the thigh and the body.

When the chicken has been cooking for about 40 minutes, toss the zucchini with the remaining olive oil and season it with salt and black pepper. Arrange the zucchini on the grill around the chicken, re-cover the kettle and cook the chicken and the zucchini for 20–25 minutes, or until the zucchini is tender, but not soggy. Put the zucchini in a serving dish and sprinkle it with the parsley. When the chicken is ready, remove it from the barbecue, cover it loosely with foil and leave it to rest for 10 minutes. Remove all the garlic from the chicken cavity but do not peel the cloves. Serve the chicken with the zucchini and garlic.

SERVES 4

Chicken and mushroom risotto

2 tablespoons olive oil
300 g (10½ oz) boneless,
    skinless chicken breasts,
    cut into thin strips
250 g (9 oz) small button
    mushrooms, halved
pinch freshly grated nutmeg
2 garlic cloves, crushed
20 g (¾ oz) butter
1 small onion, finely chopped
380 g (13½ oz/1¾ cups)
    risotto rice

170 ml (5½ fl oz/⅔ cup) dry
    white wine
1.25 litres (44 fl oz/5 cups) hot
    vegetable or chicken stock
3 tablespoons sour cream
50 g (1¾ oz/½ cup) grated
    parmesan cheese
3 tablespoons finely chopped
    flat-leaf (Italian) parsley

Heat the oil in a large saucepan. Cook the chicken pieces over high heat for 3–4 minutes, or until golden. Add the mushrooms and cook for 1–2 minutes, or until starting to brown. Stir in the nutmeg and garlic, season with salt and pepper and cook for 30 seconds. Remove from the pan.

Melt the butter in the same saucepan and cook the onion over low heat for 5–6 minutes. Add the rice, stir to coat, then stir in the wine. Once the wine is absorbed, stir in a ladleful of the hot stock and cook over medium heat, stirring continuously. When the stock has been absorbed, stir in another ladleful. Continue like this for about 20 minutes, or until all the stock has been added and the rice is creamy and *al dente*. Stir in the mushrooms and chicken with the last of the stock.

Remove the pan from the heat and stir in the sour cream, parmesan and parsley.

SERVES 4

Chicken and cider stew with apple and potato mash

1 kg (2 lb 4 oz) boneless, skinless chicken thighs, cut into bite-sized cubes
1½ tablespoons finely chopped thyme
1 tablespoon olive oil
90 g (3¼ oz) butter
3 French shallots, thinly sliced

375 ml (13 fl oz/1½ cups) alcoholic apple cider
1 kg (2 lb 4 oz) all-purpose potatoes, cubed
2 large green apples, peeled, cored and sliced into eighths
170 ml (5½ fl oz/⅔ cup) pouring (whipping) cream

Season the chicken with 2 teaspoons of the thyme and some salt and black pepper. Heat the oil and 20 g (¾ oz) of the butter in a large saucepan over medium heat. Brown the chicken in two batches for 2–3 minutes. Remove.

Add the shallots and the remaining thyme to the pan and sauté for 2 minutes. Pour in the cider, then bring to the boil, scraping off any sediment from the bottom. Return the chicken to the pan and cover. Reduce the heat to medium–low and cook for 35–40 minutes, or until the chicken is tender and the sauce has reduced (check occasionally to see if any water needs to be added).

Meanwhile, cook the potato and apple in a saucepan of boiling water for 15–20 minutes, or until tender. Drain and return to the pan over low heat for 1 minute to allow any water to evaporate. Remove from the heat, and mash with a potato masher. Stir in 2 tablespoons of the cream and the remaining butter with a wooden spoon, then season well with salt and pepper.

Stir the remaining cream into the stew and cook for another 2–4 minutes, or until the sauce has thickened. Serve at once with the potato and apple mash.

SERVES 4

Coq au vin

1 tablespoon olive oil
12 white baby onions, peeled
3 bacon slices, chopped
40 g (1½ oz) butter
1.5 kg (3 lb 5 oz) chicken pieces
    on the bone (skin on)
2 garlic cloves, crushed
375 ml (13 fl oz/1½ cups) dry
    red wine
2 tablespoons brandy

1 tablespoon chopped thyme
1 bay leaf
4 parsley stalks
250 g (9 oz) button mushrooms,
    halved
20 g (¾ oz) butter, extra,
    softened
2 tablespoons plain
    (all-purpose) flour
chopped parsley, to serve

Preheat the oven to 170°C (325°F/Gas 3). Heat the oil in a large heavy-based frying pan and add the onions. Cook until browned, then add the bacon and cook until browned. Remove the bacon and onions and add the butter to the pan. When the butter is foaming, add the chicken in batches and cook until well browned. Transfer to an ovenproof dish, draining it of any fat, then add the onions and bacon.

Tip any excess fat out of the frying pan and add the garlic, wine, brandy, thyme, bay leaf and parsley stalks. Bring to the boil, then pour over the chicken. Cook, covered, in the oven for 1½ hours, then add the mushrooms and cook for 30 minutes. Drain through a colander and reserve the liquid in a pan. Keep the chicken, bacon, onions and mushrooms warm in the oven.

Mix the softened butter and flour together, bring the liquid in the pan to the boil and whisk in the flour and butter paste in two batches, then reduce the heat and simmer until the liquid thickens slightly. Return the chicken, bacon and vegetables to the ovenproof dish. Pour in the sauce, scatter on the chopped parsley and serve.

SERVES 4

Chicken and pork paella

3 tablespoons olive oil
1 red capsicum (pepper), cut
    into 5 mm (¼ inch) wide strips
600 g (1 lb 5 oz) boneless,
    skinless chicken thighs, cut
    into bite-sized cubes
200 g (7 oz) chorizo sausage, cut
    into 2 cm (¾ inch) thick pieces
200 g (7 oz) mushrooms, thinly
    sliced
3 garlic cloves, crushed
1 tablespoon lemon zest
700 g (1 lb 9 oz) tomatoes,
    roughly chopped

200 g (7 oz) green beans,
    trimmed and cut into 3 cm
    (1¼ inch) lengths
1 tablespoon chopped rosemary
2 tablespoons chopped flat-leaf
    (Italian) parsley
¼ teaspoon saffron threads
    dissolved in 3 tablespoons
    hot water
440 g (15½ oz/2 cups) short-
    grain rice
750 ml (26 fl oz/3 cups) hot
    chicken stock
6 lemon wedges

Heat the oil in a large, deep frying pan or paella pan over medium heat. Add the capsicum and cook for 6 minutes, or until softened. Remove from the pan. Add the chicken to the pan and cook for 10 minutes, or until brown on all sides. Remove.

Add the sausage to the pan and cook for 5 minutes, or until golden on all sides. Remove from the pan.

Add the mushrooms, garlic and lemon zest, and cook over medium heat for 5 minutes. Stir in the tomato and capsicum, and cook for a further 5 minutes, or until the tomato is soft.

Add the beans, rosemary, parsley, saffron mixture, rice, chicken and sausage. Stir briefly and add the stock. Do not stir. Reduce the heat and simmer for 30 minutes. Remove from the heat, cover and leave to stand for 10 minutes. Serve with lemon.

SERVES 6

Green chicken, bean and broccoli curry

Curry paste

½ teaspoon cumin seeds

1 teaspoon coriander seeds

¼ teaspoon white peppercorns

5 coriander (cilantro) roots

3 tablespoons chopped fresh galangal

10 long green chillies, chopped

1 lemongrass stem, white part only, chopped

6 red Asian shallots

3 garlic cloves, peeled

1 tablespoon shrimp paste

1 teaspoon grated lime zest

2 tablespoons oil

250 ml (9 fl oz/1 cup) thick coconut cream

500 g (1 lb 2 oz) boneless, skinless chicken thighs, sliced

500 ml (17 fl oz/2 cups) coconut milk

125 g (4½ oz) beans, cut into 3 cm (1¼ inch) lengths

150 g (5½ oz) broccoli, cut into small florets

1 tablespoon grated palm sugar (jaggery) or soft brown sugar

2–3 tablespoons fish sauce

5 tablespoons chopped coriander (cilantro) leaves

To make the curry paste, toast the cumin and coriander seeds, then grind them and the peppercorns into a fine powder. Put the powder in a food processor with ¼ teaspoon salt and the remaining paste ingredients and process until smooth.

Put the coconut cream in a wok, bring to the boil and cook for 10 minutes, or until the oil separates. Stir in half the curry paste and cook for 3 minutes. Add the chicken in batches and cook for 4 minutes, or until almost cooked. Return all the chicken to the wok. Stir in the coconut milk, beans and broccoli. Bring to the boil, then reduce to a simmer for 10 minutes. Stir in the remaining ingredients. Serve with rice.

SERVES 4

Mediterranean
chicken stew

1 teaspoon ground cumin

1 teaspoon ground coriander

1 teaspoon paprika

¼ teaspoon ground ginger

1.5 kg (3 lb 5 oz) boneless, skinless chicken thighs, quartered

2 tablespoons olive oil

1 large onion, sliced

3 garlic cloves, finely chopped

2 teaspoons oregano, chopped

250 ml (9 fl oz/1 cup) dry white wine

300 ml (10½ fl oz) chicken stock

400 g (14 oz) tin chopped tomatoes

2 bay leaves, crushed

¼ teaspoon saffron threads, soaked in 2 tablespoons warm water

3 tablespoons each pitted green and black olives

½ preserved lemon, flesh removed and zest cut into fine slivers

3 tablespoons finely chopped flat-leaf (Italian) parsley

Combine the cumin, coriander, paprika and ginger, and rub over the chicken pieces. Heat the oil in a large saucepan. Add the chicken in batches and cook over medium heat for 5 minutes, or until browned. Remove from the pan.

Reduce the heat, add the onion and cook, stirring constantly, for 5 minutes, or until golden. Add the garlic and oregano, and cook for 2 minutes, then add the wine and cook for 6 minutes, or until nearly evaporated. Add the stock, tomato, bay leaves and saffron and soaking liquid, and bring to the boil. Return the chicken to the pan, reduce the heat and simmer, covered, for 30 minutes, or until the chicken is cooked.

Stir in the olives and lemon, and cook for 10 minutes. Remove the bay leaf, add the parsley and serve.

SERVES 4–6

Moroccan chicken

1 tablespoon Moroccan spice blend
800 g (1 lb 12 oz) boneless, skinless chicken thighs, halved
1 tablespoon olive oil
40 g (1½ oz) butter
1 large onion, cut into wedges
1 cinnamon stick
2 garlic cloves, crushed
2 tablespoons lemon juice
250 ml (9 fl oz/1 cup) chicken stock
4 tablespoons pitted prunes, halved

Sprinkle half the spice blend over the chicken and set aside for 20 minutes.

Heat the oil and 20 g (¾ oz) of the butter in a large saucepan or deep-sided frying pan over medium heat. Cook the chicken in two batches for 5 minutes each batch, or until evenly browned. Remove the chicken from the pan. Add the onion and cinnamon stick to the pan and cook for 2–3 minutes before adding the garlic. Return all the chicken to the pan and add the lemon juice and the remaining spice blend. Season, then cook, covered, for 8 minutes.

Add the stock and prunes to the pan and slowly bring to the boil. Reduce the heat to medium–low and cook, uncovered, for 15 minutes, or until the chicken is cooked and the liquid has reduced to a sauce. Before serving, stir the remaining butter into the sauce until it is melted. Serve with couscous.

SERVES 4

Pulao with fried onions and spiced chicken

4 tablespoons oil
6 cardamom pods
2 x 5 cm (2 inch) piece
   cinnamon stick
3 cloves
8 black peppercorns
260 g (9¼ oz/1⅓ cups) basmati
   rice
1 litre (35 fl oz/4 cups) hot
   chicken stock
2 handfuls coriander (cilantro)
   leaves

1 large onion, thinly sliced
2 teaspoons curry paste (any
   type)
1 tablespoon tomato paste
   (concentrated purée)
2 tablespoons yoghurt
400 g (14 oz) boneless, skinless
   chicken breasts, cut into strips
thick natural yoghurt, to serve
mango chutney, to serve

Heat 1 tablespoon of the oil over medium heat in a large heavy-based saucepan. Add the cardamom, cinnamon, cloves and peppercorns and fry for 1 minute. Reduce the heat to low, add the rice and stir constantly for 1 minute. Add the stock and some salt and quickly bring to the boil. Cover the pan and simmer over low heat for 15 minutes. Leave to stand for 10 minutes, then stir in the coriander.

Heat 2 tablespoons of the oil in a frying pan and fry the onion until it is very soft. Increase the heat and keep frying until the onion turns dark brown. Drain the onion on crumpled paper towels, then add it to the rice.

Mix the curry paste, tomato paste and yoghurt together, then add the chicken. Heat the remaining oil in a frying pan. Cook the chicken for about 4 minutes over high heat until almost black in parts. Serve the rice with the chicken, yoghurt and chutney.

SERVES 4

Hearty chicken and vegetable soup

1.5 kg (3 lb 5 oz) whole chicken
1 onion
2 large leeks, white part only,
    halved lengthways and well
    washed
3 large celery stalks
5 black peppercorns
1 bay leaf
2 large carrots, peeled and diced

1 large swede (rutabaga),
    peeled and diced
2 large tomatoes, peeled,
    seeded and finely chopped
165 g (5¾ oz/¾ cup) barley
1 tablespoon tomato paste
    (concentrated purée)
2 tablespoons finely chopped
    flat-leaf (Italian) parsley

Put the chicken, onion, 1 leek, 1 celery stalk, halved, the peppercorns and bay leaf in a large saucepan and add enough water to cover. Bring to the boil, then reduce the heat and simmer for 1½ hours, skimming any impurities that rise to the surface.

Strain the stock through a fine sieve and return to the cleaned pan. Discard the onion, leek, celery, peppercorns and bay leaf, and set the chicken aside. When the chicken is cool enough to handle, discard the fat and bones, then shred the flesh, cover and refrigerate until needed.

Allow the stock to cool, then refrigerate overnight. Skim the fat from the surface, put the stock in a large saucepan and bring to the boil. Dice the remaining leek and celery and add to the soup with the carrot, swede, tomato, barley and tomato paste. Simmer for 45–50 minutes, or until the vegetables are cooked and the barley is tender. Stir in the parsley and shredded chicken. Simmer until warmed through, then season to taste before serving.

SERVES 4–6

Chicken and leek pies

60 g (2¼ oz) butter
1 leek, white part only, thinly sliced
4 boneless, skinless chicken breasts, cut into bite-sized cubes
50 g (1¾ oz) plain (all-purpose) flour
250 ml (9 fl oz/1 cup) chicken stock
300 ml (10½ fl oz) pouring (whipping) cream
150 g (5½ oz/1 cup) fresh or frozen peas, blanched
1 sheet ready-rolled puff pastry, thawed

Melt the butter in a saucepan over medium heat and cook the leek for 2–3 minutes, or until soft. Add the chicken and cook for 4–5 minutes, or until cooked. Add the flour and cook, stirring, until it starts to bubble. Add the stock and cook until the mixture starts to thicken. Add the cream, reserving 1 tablespoon to glaze the pastry. Cook until the mixture just starts to boil. Stir in the peas. Season. Remove from the heat. Preheat the oven to 200°C (400°F/Gas 6).

Divide the filling among four individual pie dishes or ramekins. Top with a circle of pastry, cut just bigger than the top of the dish, then press around the edges to seal. Brush the surface with the reserved cream. Make a small slit in the top to allow steam to escape. Place the dishes on a metal tray and bake for 20–25 minutes, or until the pastry is golden. Serve with a green salad.

SERVES 4

Spanish-style
chicken casserole

2 tablespoons light olive oil

750 g (1 lb 10 oz) chicken thighs on the bone (skin on)

750 g (1 lb 10 oz) chicken drumsticks

1 large onion, chopped

2 garlic cloves, crushed

2 teaspoons sweet paprika

1 large red capsicum (pepper), sliced

200 ml (7 fl oz) dry sherry

400 g (14 oz) tin whole peeled tomatoes

2 tablespoons tomato paste (concentrated purée)

175 g (6 oz/1 cup) green olives, pitted, halved

1 teaspoon sweet paprika, extra, to garnish

Preheat the oven to 180°C (350°F/Gas 4). Heat the oil in a large frying pan, add the chicken in batches and cook over medium heat for 3–4 minutes, or until browned. Transfer to a 4 litre (140 fl oz/16 cup) flameproof casserole dish. Add the onion, garlic, paprika and capsicum to the frying pan, and cook for 5–8 minutes, or until softened. Add the sherry and cook for 2 minutes, or until slightly reduced. Add the tomatoes and tomato paste, stir well and cook for 2 minutes. Pour the tomato mixture over the chicken and add 250 ml (9 fl oz/1 cup) water.

Bake, covered, for 1¼ hours, then uncovered for 15 minutes. Add the olives and leave for 10 minutes. Garnish with the extra paprika and serve with rice.

SERVES 4

Malaysian Nonya chicken curry

Curry paste

2 red onions, chopped

4 small red chillies, seeded and sliced

4 garlic cloves, sliced

2 lemongrass stems, white part only, sliced

2 x 3 cm (¾ x 1¼ inch) piece fresh galangal, sliced

8 makrut (kaffir lime) leaves, roughly chopped

1 teaspoon ground turmeric

½ teaspoon shrimp paste, dry-roasted

2 tablespoons oil

750 g (1 lb 10 oz) boneless, skinless chicken thighs, cut into bite-sized pieces

400 ml (14 fl oz) coconut milk

3 tablespoons tamarind purée

1 tablespoon fish sauce

3 makrut (kaffir lime) leaves, shredded

To make the curry paste, put all of the ingredients in a food processor or blender and process to a thick paste.

Heat a wok to hot, add the oil and swirl to coat the side. Add the curry paste and cook, stirring occasionally, over low heat for 8–10 minutes, or until fragrant. Add the chicken and stir-fry with the paste for 2–3 minutes.

Add the coconut milk, tamarind purée and fish sauce to the wok, and simmer, stirring occasionally, for 15–20 minutes, or until the chicken is tender. Garnish with the lime leaves. Serve with rice and steamed bok choy (pak choy).

SERVES 4

NOTE: Use a non-stick or stainless steel wok to cook this recipe because the tamarind purée will react with the metal in a regular wok and will taint the dish.

Jambalaya

1 tablespoon olive oil

2 boneless, skinless chicken breasts, cut into thin strips

1 red onion, sliced

3 bacon slices, chopped

2 chorizo sausages, cut into 1 cm (½ inch) thick slices on the diagonal

1 small red capsicum (pepper), sliced

1 small green capsicum (pepper), sliced

2 garlic cloves, finely chopped

1–2 teaspoons seeded, finely chopped jalapeño chilli

1 teaspoon smoked paprika

3 teaspoons Cajun spice mix

400 g (14 oz/2 cups) long-grain rice, washed

250 ml (9 fl oz/1 cup) beer

4 vine-ripened tomatoes, peeled and quartered

750 ml (26 fl oz/3 cups) chicken stock

½ teaspoon saffron threads, soaked in 1 tablespoon warm water

16 raw medium prawns (shrimp), peeled and deveined, tails intact

Heat the oil in a large saucepan. Cook the chicken in batches over medium heat for 4 minutes, or until lightly browned. Remove.

Cook the onion for 3 minutes, then add the bacon and sausage, and cook for 4–5 minutes, or until browned. Add the capsicum and cook for 2 minutes, then add the garlic, chilli, paprika and Cajun spice mix, and cook for a further 2 minutes.

Add the rice and stir to coat. Add the beer and stir for 30 seconds to remove any sediment stuck to the pan. Stir in the tomato, stock, saffron and soaking liquid. Bring to the boil, reduce the heat and simmer, covered, for 10–12 minutes.

Add the prawns and chicken, stir to prevent sticking, and cook, covered, for 3–5 minutes, or until the rice is creamy and tender. Serve immediately.

SERVES 6

Baked chicken and leek risotto

60 g (2¼ oz) butter
1 leek, white part only, thinly sliced
2 boneless, skinless chicken breasts, cut into bite-sized cubes
440 g (15½ oz/2 cups) risotto rice
3 tablespoons dry white wine
1.25 litres (44 fl oz/5 cups) chicken stock
4 tablespoons grated parmesan cheese, plus extra, to serve
2 tablespoons thyme, plus extra, to serve

Preheat the oven to 150°C (300°F/Gas 2) and put an ovenproof dish with a lid in the oven to heat up.

Heat the butter in a saucepan over medium heat, stir in the leek and cook for about 2 minutes, then add the chicken and stir for 3 minutes. Toss in the rice and stir for 1 minute. Add the wine and stock, and bring to the boil.

Pour into the ovenproof dish and cover. Cook in the oven for 30 minutes, stirring halfway through. Remove from the oven and stir in the cheese and thyme. Season, then sprinkle with extra thyme and cheese before serving.

SERVES 4

Chicken, artichoke and broad bean stew

150 g (5½ oz/1 cup) frozen broad (fava) beans
8 chicken thighs on the bone (see Note)
60 g (2¼ oz/½ cup) seasoned plain (all-purpose) flour
2 tablespoons olive oil
1 large red onion, cut into small wedges
125 ml (4 fl oz/½ cup) dry white wine
250 ml (9 fl oz/1 cup) chicken stock
2 teaspoons finely chopped rosemary
330 g (11¾ oz/1½ cups) quartered marinated
    artichokes, well drained

Remove the skins from the broad beans. Coat the chicken in the flour, shaking off the excess. Heat the oil in a large saucepan or flameproof casserole dish, then brown the chicken in two batches on all sides over medium heat. Remove and drain on crumpled paper towels.

Add the onion to the pan and cook for 3–4 minutes, or until soft but not brown. Increase the heat to high, pour in the wine and boil for 2 minutes, or until reduced to a syrup. Stir in the stock and bring just to the boil, then return the chicken to the saucepan with the rosemary. Reduce the heat to low and simmer, covered, for 45 minutes. Add the artichokes, increase the heat to high and return to the boil. Reduce to a simmer and cook, uncovered, for 10–15 minutes. Add the beans and cook for 5 minutes. Serve with mashed potato.

SERVES 4

NOTE: If you prefer, remove the skin from the chicken.

Chicken and corn pies

1 tablespoon olive oil
650 g (1 lb 7 oz) boneless,
    skinless chicken thighs, cut
    into 1 cm (½ inch) cubes
1 tablespoon grated fresh ginger
400 g (14 oz) oyster mushrooms,
    halved
3 corn cobs, kernels removed
125 ml (4 fl oz/½ cup) chicken
    stock

2 tablespoons kecap manis
2 tablespoons cornflour
    (cornstarch)
2 large handfuls coriander
    (cilantro) leaves, chopped
6 sheets ready-rolled shortcrust
    (pie) pastry
milk, to glaze

Grease six metal pie tins measuring 9.5 cm (3¾ inches) on the base and 3 cm (1¼ inches) deep. Heat the oil in a large frying pan over high heat and add the chicken. Cook for 5 minutes, or until golden. Add the ginger, mushrooms and corn kernels and cook for 5–6 minutes, or until the chicken is just cooked through. Add the stock and kecap manis.

Mix the cornflour with 2 tablespoons water in a small bowl, then stir into the pan. Boil for 2 minutes before adding the coriander. Transfer to a bowl, cool a little, then refrigerate for 2 hours, or until cold.

Preheat the oven to 180°C (350°F/Gas 4). Using a saucer to guide you, cut a 15 cm (6 inch) round from each sheet of shortcrust pastry and line the six pie tins. Fill the shells with the cooled filling, then cut out another six rounds large enough to make the lids. Top the pies with the lids, cut away any extra pastry and seal the edges with a fork. Decorate the pies with shapes cut from pastry scraps. Prick a few holes in the top of each pie, brush with a little milk and bake for 35 minutes, or until golden. Serve with a salad.

MAKES 6

Chicken, broccoli and pasta bake

300 g (10½ oz) fusilli
425 g (15 oz) tin cream of mushroom soup
2 eggs
185 g (6½ oz/¾ cup) whole-egg mayonnaise
1 tablespoon dijon mustard
210 g (7½ oz/1⅔ cups) grated cheddar cheese
600 g (1 lb 5 oz) boneless, skinless chicken breasts, thinly sliced
400 g (14 oz) frozen broccoli pieces, thawed
40 g (1½ oz/½ cup) fresh breadcrumbs

Preheat the oven to 180°C (350°F/Gas 4). Cook the pasta in a large saucepan of boiling salted water until *al dente*, then drain and return to the pan. Combine the soup, eggs, mayonnaise, mustard and half the cheese in a bowl.

Heat a lightly greased non-stick frying pan over medium heat, add the chicken pieces and cook for 5–6 minutes, or until cooked through. Season with salt and pepper, then set aside to cool.

Add the chicken and broccoli to the pasta, pour the soup mixture over the top and stir until well combined. Transfer the mixture to a 3 litre (105 fl oz/12 cup) ovenproof dish. Sprinkle with the combined breadcrumbs and remaining cheese. Bake for 20 minutes, or until the top is golden brown. Serve with a salad.

SERVES 6–8

Chicken casserole with mustard and tarragon sauce

3 tablespoons olive oil

1 kg (2 lb 4 oz) boneless, skinless
  chicken thighs, halved, then
  quartered

1 onion, finely chopped

1 leek, white part only, sliced

1 garlic clove, finely chopped

350 g (12 oz) button
  mushrooms, sliced

½ teaspoon dried tarragon

375 ml (13 fl oz/1½ cups)
  chicken stock

185 ml (6 fl oz/¾ cup) pouring
  (whipping) cream

2 teaspoons lemon juice

2 teaspoons dijon mustard

Preheat the oven to 180°C (350°F/Gas 4). Heat 1 tablespoon of the oil in a flameproof casserole dish over medium heat, and cook the chicken in two batches for 6–7 minutes each, or until golden. Remove from the dish and set aside.

Add the remaining oil to the dish and cook the onion, leek and garlic over medium heat for 5 minutes, or until soft. Add the mushrooms and cook for 5–7 minutes, or until they are soft and browned, and most of the liquid has evaporated. Add the tarragon, chicken stock, cream, lemon juice and mustard, bring to the boil and cook for 2 minutes. Return the chicken pieces to the dish and season well. Cover.

Put the casserole in the oven and cook for 1 hour, or until the sauce has reduced and thickened. Season to taste, and serve with boiled new potatoes and a green salad.

SERVES 4

index

First published in 2009 by Murdoch Books Pty Limited

Murdoch Books Australia
Pier 8/9, 23 Hickson Road
Millers Point NSW 2000
Phone: +61 (0) 2 8220 2000
Fax: +61 (0) 2 8220 2558
www.murdochbooks.com.au

Murdoch Books UK Limited
Erico House, 6th Floor
93–99 Upper Richmond Road,
Putney, London SW15 2TG
Phone: +44 (0) 20 8785 5995
Fax: +44 (0) 20 8785 5985
www.murdochbooks.co.uk

Chief Executive: Juliet Rogers
Publishing Director: Kay Scarlett

Design manager: Vivien Valk
Project manager: Gordana Trifunovic
Editor: Zoë Harpham
Design concept: Alex Frampton
Designer: Susanne Geppert
Production: Alexandra Gonzalez
Recipes developed by the Murdoch Books Test Kitchen

Printed by Sing Cheong Printing Co. Ltd in 2009. PRINTED IN HONG KONG.
National Library of Australia Cataloguing-in-Publication Data
    Chicken. Includes index.
    ISBN 978 1 74196 3786 (pbk).
    1. Cookery (Chicken) (Series: Test kitchen) 641.665

IMPORTANT: Those who might be at risk from the effects of salmonella poisoning (the
elderly, pregnant women, young children and those suffering from immune deficiency
diseases) should consult their doctor with any concerns about eating raw eggs.

CONVERSION GUIDE: You may find cooking times vary depending on the oven you
are using. For fan-forced ovens, as a general rule, set the oven temperature to 20°C (35°F)
lower than indicated in the recipe. We have used 20 ml (4 teaspoon) tablespoon measures.
If you are using a 15 ml (3 teaspoon) tablespoon, for most recipes the difference will not
be noticeable. However, for recipes using baking powder, gelatine, bicarbonate of soda
(baking soda), small amounts of flour and cornflour (cornstarch), add an extra teaspoon
for each tablespoon specified.